THE STRANGER
IN OUR HOUSE

THE STRANGER IN OUR HOUSE

Growing Up With Holocaust Survivors—
A Memoir

Kathy Hoffstadter-Thal

Donnybrook Publishing

Copyright © 2011 by Kathy Hoffstadter-Thal

Photography courtesy of Kathy Hoffstadter-Thal collection unless otherwise credited

Cover Design by Accurance
Interior Design by Day to Day Enterprises
Edited by Maureen Buchanan Jones, Samantha Dias
      and Marion Landew

ISBN: 978-0-9833965-0-5
eISBN: 978-0-9833965-1-2
Printed in the United States of America
10 9 8 7 6 5 4 3 2 1

Library of Congress Control Number: 2011937936

Publisher's Cataloging-in-Publication data available upon request

Published by Donnybrook Publishing •Demarest, NJ
http://www.DonnybrookPublishing.com

For Boreshka and Artur

PREFACE

The writing that follows took place over nineteen years of my adult life, starting with the birth of my first son, Adam. I am hopeful that writing this book will act as a catharsis for the many painful childhood memories that I harbor. I also hope this book will shed some light on the suffering of children who grew up in the homes of Holocaust survivors and the homes of those struggling with mental illness.

The Stranger in Our House has been a journey, which has gone through several transformations. I started from the perspective of a child of Holocaust survivors, dealing with my parents' trauma and the empathy I felt toward them. I felt a compelling obligation to make concrete the trauma that my family had experienced at the hands of the Nazis. As the book developed, anger and resentment rose within me, with the realization of having grown up in a severely dysfunctional home and of having a father with mental illness. Toward the end, I uncovered family secrets that are both joyous and heart wrenching.

ACKNOWLEDGEMENTS

I would like to thank the many people who have guided and encouraged me to bring this endeavor to fruition. Firstly, I would like to thank Marion Landew, who edited my memoir in the rawest of forms and encouraged me to move forward with publication. To Dr. Sophia Richman for her insightful contribution as a holocaust survivor, author and psychologist. To Dr. Irit Felsen, for her sensitivity and sensibility as both a child of holocaust survivors and a psychologist with experience in holocaust trauma. To my friends and family, Randi Weiss, Bambi Fisher, Jill and Maury Buchalter, Myra and Yosef Levi, Debbie Slevin, David Oberman, Ruth Heber, Olga Greenspan, Susan Thal and Elizabeth Friedman. To my adored sons, Adam, David and Jonathan and to my husband Gary who are the sunshine of my life. All of you have encouraged me along the way and found the right words to propel me when I was doubtful.

To Rochelle Rubinstein, for her passion and devotion in reviewing and editing my manuscript and for the tireless hours of feedback she provided. The final product is much enhanced because of her efforts.

To Maureen Buchanan Jones, my developmental editor from Full Tilt Writing, whose professionalism, honesty and kindness helped bring this book to a higher level. To Samantha Dias, of Making Words Shine, my copyeditor, whose literary talent, encouragement and positive feedback I was privileged to receive and to Nora Liu of Quest Technology, Inc. for her translation service. To MyLinda Butterworth of Day to Day Enterprises for her time and patience in the interior book design.

Lastly, to Shel Horowitz, from Frugal Marketing, who orchestrated all aspects of the book publishing process. Without Shel's professional guidance and help finding editors, cover artists and book printers this manuscript would still be sitting on my desk.

INTRODUCTION

I am the youngest of three children whose parents were Hungarian Jewish Holocaust survivors. My mother, whom I adored and loved more than I could imagine any child loving a parent, was kind, loving, and empathetic. Her only fault was in accepting her destiny and never questioning her fate. She took what was handed to her, including the cruel, callous indifference of my father, the man she married.

For many years, I believed that my father's narcissistic and sadistic ways had resulted from his experiences during the Holocaust. But, after seeing many loving, caring parents who had also suffered at the hands of the Nazis, I pondered whether my father may have had prior intrinsic aberrations that made him the heartless person he was. It has been said that apes, unlike humans, lack the higher-level brain functions of empathy and altruism. I wondered if my father, like apes, lacked these gifts of evolution as well or if his character had been altered by the traumas he had experienced during the Holocaust.

As a child and as a young adult, I engaged in a futile attempt to normalize my father. My encounters with him showed that he neither loved nor cared for me in the way that a parent should love and care for a child. I cared for him. I relentlessly gave of myself to keep my father content so that he would not terrorize our family, our friends, and our neighbors. I did what I felt I had to do to tame him. I believed that no one else in the family was willing—or able—to make this effort. With no one else in control, I felt obliged to be my father's parent, child, companion, and therapist. I was my father's keeper.

My father lived in a regimented world of systems and order that only he could understand. This world revolved around him, and only he was of significance. What didn't benefit him was of little interest, including the members of our family. He gave nothing, yet he expected alot in return. With him in our midst, there were almost no happy moments for my mother, sister, brother, and me. I was repulsed, sickened, and absolutely petrified of my father nearly all the time. But occasionally, I felt sorry for him, for his losses, and for what he had experienced at the hands of the Nazis.

My father's behavior and character created an impenetrable barrier around our family and around me. Being Jewish and the child of Holocaust survivors meant being different, but being my father's daughter meant being apart from everything.

From as far back as my conscious memory takes me, these feelings of being different from other children existed. I understood that something tragic and terrible had happened to my family. Although I did not live through the experiences of the Holocaust, its demons had permeated my soul. My mother, Luiza Rothfeld, known in Hungarian as Luizi, spent a year in ghettos and concentration camps. My father, Laszlo Hofstadter, known in Hungarian as Laci, escaped from the cattle car on which he was being deported only hours before the train's arrival at Auschwitz.

I spent years trying to understand it all. There were so many questions with so few answers. How could six million Jews vanish off the face of the earth? How could people be tormented, tortured, and murdered solely because of their religion? How could so many people knowingly have allowed this to happen? Most of all, how could God have allowed this to happen? Could there be a God if such things could happen?

It was incomprehensible. I wanted desperately to wipe it out of my mind. The feelings, thoughts, visions, and horrors I couldn't understand lay dormant in my memory for short periods of time, only to surface again. Why did I think about them all the time? Why couldn't I suppress them, as I learned one was supposed to do with uncomfortable emotions? I wanted to put it all away in my unconscious to never return, but it never worked out that way. I thought about it all the time.

Until I was in my early thirties, a day rarely passed without my having a thought, a vision, or tears associated with the Holocaust. I imagined concentration camps, hunger, disease, terrible pain, and suffering. I envisioned over and over again the image of my mother's mother and siblings taking their last steps toward the gas chambers. There were visions of naked humans asking God *Why?* as they took their last breaths. There were visions of people clinging to one another in their struggle for survival. I wondered when the scenes would stop, and I feared they never would. I was haunted by the traumatic events of my parents' past.

Throughout childhood, and even into young adulthood, much of the happiness in my life was derived from helping my parents find contentment. I felt solely responsible for their happiness. Only if they were happy could I be happy. I desperately wanted to make up for their losses, and I often found myself living through their emotions.

What I didn't realize was that this mission could never be accomplished. The wounds were too deep, the scars too thick. My parents brought with them an underlying misery from the war. It was a part of their lives.

The driving force behind my accomplishments was to satisfy them. I had a dire need for their happiness. When I was sad, I thought about the heartache my parents and others had experienced and were still experiencing. I imagined their faces and felt their emotions. When I was hungry, I thought about their hunger. When I was in pain, I thought about their pain. When I felt happy, I felt guilty for the happiness that had been denied them. I found myself fasting on days such as Yom Kippur, not for the true religious meaning of the holidays, but to challenge myself the way my family had been challenged so that I could come close to feeling the same pain. It never stopped.

As a Jew, I believed that the world would never be a safe place for me or my family. I was on constant guard against anti-Semitic actions. I believed that Jews would always be targets of hatred. History would repeat itself. Not *if*, but *when*. It was only a matter of time. When I heard about an anti-Semitic event, my first thought was how close it was geographically to me, and then I tried to convince myself that it was not a local phenomenon. When I read about skinheads or neo-Nazis, I would contemplate strategic maneuvers to protect my family. Where could we go? Did I look Jewish? Was my name Jewish? Was it wrong to give my sons names like Adam, David, and Jonathan? Would my sons be identified as Jews because they were circumcised? Was it a mistake to put the mezuzah on the door? Could my father be right after all? I feared for the Hasidim, who were so overtly Jewish, yet I envied their courage.

I'm not sure how I first learned of the Holocaust, considering that my parents didn't talk about it much.

As a matter of fact, my parents didn't talk much at all to us children, and they were especially silent among themselves. There was little chance to overhear a conversation. On the rare occasion when my parents did speak to each other, it was in Hungarian, which I did not understand. I grew up with sparse information. What I knew was mostly from television and photographs.

We spent a few minutes on the Holocaust in history class during my senior year of high school. I left the classroom and headed straight for the bathroom door on the day that the history teacher, Mr. Held, began discussing the subject. "Today we will learn about the Holocaust" meant "Exit stage left" for me. I could not bear to listen, and the possibility of seeing photographs was unimaginable. Movies were out of the question. I vowed never to watch anything associated with the Holocaust. Catching a few minutes of a documentary on the concentration camps while switching channels would leave me tormented for the rest of the night and sometimes even for several days later.

But as I grew older, I wanted to learn more and tell my parents' story for the sake of testimony. It was clear to me that when speaking to my parents, there was an unspoken agreement that I could carefully touch on certain topics, but others were forbidden. I felt the need to make the memory of each of my grandparents, aunts, and uncles, whom I had never known, materialize into more than "one of the six million Jews." I needed to give each of them an identity. They could not just simply vanish without a trace. I also wanted to let others know how we, the children of Holocaust survivors, have suffered along with our parents—many of whom were so traumatized by their experience that they passed their trauma on to their children. I deeply hope that my children and their children will be spared this dark cloud.

Capturing my parents' Holocaust story was not easy. During my thirties and forties, for the first time, I gingerly questioned them and gauged how far I could go. I spent countless hours writing little bits of information on whatever was handy at the moment: a piece of scrap paper, a paper cup, a napkin, or a sticky note. I feared that if my parents felt they were being interviewed, they wouldn't talk. Actually, my father didn't talk much at all, and he especially didn't talk about those years or his family. His response to questions was usually "One day, I will tell you." He had perfected the art of evasiveness.

My mother, in her dying days, gifted me with her participation in the *Survivors of the Shoah*, a video collection generously funded by the actor and film producer, Steven Spielberg. She clearly had not wanted to give her personal testimony for the video archive, but she knew it meant a great deal to me to have her story, so she consented to be interviewed. The interview was conducted in Hungarian. The video sat on my bookshelf for seven years until I met a Hungarian woman named Olga Greenspan. Through a friend of Olga's, Nora Liu of

Quest Technology, Inc., Olga had the video translated, and I was given a written transcript, much of which is included in these pages. I have written my parents' stories of the events that led up to the war as well as their experiences during the war and afterwards in their own voices.

2007

It is almost ten thirty when I arrive at his apartment, schlepping his weekly goods. I can still feel the stress from my morning escapade at the local A&P supermarket that had contributed to my tardy arrival. The A&P was out of Poland Spring water with the handle. I had carefully considered breaking his ritual and buying the one without the handle. Already late, I chose the handleless bottle and concocted the justification of the purchase in my mind. I headed to the dairy section. *What! No Dannon peach yogurt?* I cursed the A&P for their ineptness as I realized that I would have to stop at another supermarket along the way.

I knock on the door and wonder if he will be upset because of the delay. I relax a little, and I remind myself that he has been less agitated lately since starting the antidepressant.

"Who is it?" he asked.

"It's me," I responded.

I stand outside his door for several minutes as I hear him shuffling back and forth, sorting what he needs to sort to have things in just the right place before he lets me in. Finally, I hear the familiar screech as he pulls the kitchen chair he uses as a doorstop away from the door.

"Hi, Daddy."

I cringe as I kiss him hello. I am repulsed by the physical contact but relieved by the expression on his face. His face is relaxed, and he has made eye contact with me. Today I will not be dismissed, rejected, or leave feeling guilty. I can now start to relax.

"I am so happy that you are back," he says.

We have just returned from helping Adam move in for his first year at The University of Wisconsin.

I close the door, and two empty water bottles that have been tied to the doorknob for added security clang together. In the background, the Christian radio station that my father calls "The Family Radio Station" plays loudly from his bedroom, saying something about following the word of Jesus and his disciples. I walk past the padlocked refrigerator and find a place to sit amid the densely packed furniture in a room that long ago took on the appearance of a thrift shop. Over the two years since he moved into the independent living facility, my father has moved all the furniture closer and closer to the center of the 200-square-foot living room. The perimeter of the room is four to five feet of empty space.

"Daddy, you've moved everything to the middle of the room. It's too cluttered, and you barely have a path to walk. It's not safe. You could fall."

"The air conditioner needs room to circulate the air," he explains. "There can't be anything blocking it."

When he goes to the bathroom, I quickly move a rickety bookshelf and a 1970s red velvet chair back toward the wall. I try to move things back a little—praying that they don't break—but I know it's of no use because he will notice and move it all back again. Since my last visit, he has marked the floor eight inches in front of the refrigerator with a permanent marker so that he knows exactly how far it should stick out.

I sit for a few minutes of conversation. Because of his good mood, I feel almost giddy. I marvel at his storytelling abilities, memory, and mastery of the fine details of both current and past events. He speaks passionately about Beethoven and the recent autobiographies he has read. He walks over to his desk and picks up a CD case.

"This is what I would like for my birthday. Mozart's Piano Concerto no. 21 in C Major. It is my favorite, but I want exactly the same one with the same cover."

"If you already have one, then why do you want another?"

"It's better to have two. It's not a big deal. You can probably find it at Kmart."

This request will set me on another hunt for what he wants, exactly as he wants it. But it will be for his birthday, so I move on.

Sometimes our conversations feel almost normal.

"I just finished *The Good Earth*," I say, knowing Pearl Buck is one of his favorite authors and it will please him.

"It is one of my favorite books," he says.

I can sense that we are connecting, and the strain of our pressured conversation is beginning to ease. Over the years, he has been an avid reader, especially of autobiographies.

"Yes, how did you like it?"

"I liked it a lot. It was simple but good literature," I answer.

"It was written by Pearl Buck," he says. "You know I read Pearl Buck's autobiography, *My Several Worlds.* She was the daughter of a missionary and grew up in China. In this book, she says, 'Little boys are like dynamite.'" He chuckles after he says this, and I wonder if he is referring to himself or to my brother. Another interesting book she wrote is *Peony.* It's about the Jewish people in China," he continues. "For hundreds of years, the Chinese did not know about Jesus, so there was no anti-Semitism, so the Jews of China had a good opportunity to assimilate."

He gets up from his kitchen chair and shuffles back to his desk, barely lifting his shoes off the ground as he walks.

"Can you show me how to use the new remote?" he asks.

"Sure," I say.

He reaches into his pocket and pulls out his wallet. I watch as he carefully removes four rubber bands that circle his wallet. He takes out a key and unlocks the padlock on his desk. He removes another key to unlock the individual drawers. He pulls out a little package and removes the rubber bands around it along with the wax paper individually wrapping two AA batteries, which he gently places into the remote control.

I show him how to use the remote, and I prepare his medications for the week. I have spent my obligatory hour, and I can now go.

"I'll be leaving now," I announce as I cower, waiting for his disappointment.

"Wait, let me look at my list first," he responds as he pulls out his little piece of paper where he has written meticulous details for our conversation, his shopping list, and what he will need to give me. I wait for him to methodically go through his notes. I am getting agitated.

"Did you buy the yogurt?" he asks, as he begins his ritual confirmation, checking his list against what I have brought.

Refusing to revisit the interrogations of my childhood, I say, "Everything is there. I'm not going over the list with you."

"OK, that's it," he announces.

My body stiffens again as I kiss him goodbye. I walk out the door for my quick getaway. I take a deep breath, and I scurry down the hall, feeling released from captivity. I am halfway down the hall when his door opens. My agitation rises. I wish I had walked just a little faster; maybe I would have already been out of sight.

He calls after me, "Keti, Keti, wait! You forgot something."

"What?" I call back to him, reaching my threshold for tolerance.

"Your pen," he says.

"Keep it!" I yell back down the hall as I break away.

MY MOTHER

My parents were both from Hungary. My father, Laszlo Hofstadter, was born in a town called Kishkunhalas and moved to Nagyteteni, a town along the Danube river outside of Budapest when he was seven. My mother, Luiza Rothfeld, was born in a small town on the Hungarian-Czechoslovakian border called Ausztely (Oste) in Bereg County, located about six kilometers from Beregszasz. The town belonged to Czechoslovakia until 1938. In 1938, it was occupied by Hungary. This is my mother's story, compiled mostly from the stories she told me over the years, supplemented by the video she did for Spielberg, and told in her own words.

⧼⧽

I, Luizi Rothfeld, came from an Orthodox family of eight children. Five girls: Gizi, me, Boreshka, Reli, and Molvin. Three boys: Sanyi (from my father's first marriage to Ilonka, who died when Sanyi was a few years old), Miklosh, and Emil. My family had four additional children who died in childhood: Saren, born in 1923, died from an unknown illness at the age of thirteen; Erno, born in 1924, also died young from an unknown illness; and twin girls, Margaret and Helen, died from what people called "lack of mother's milk."

In Ausztely, my family lived on farmland given to my father, David Rothfeld, and his three brothers (Farkosh, Hermosh, and a third brother who died during World War I and whose name I do not know) by their father, Mendel Rothfeld. The entire town was two streets. We lived on Main Street in a one-family house with a grocery store in the front where we sold milk from our cows and produce from our land. We grew wheat, corn, and potatoes; raised chickens; and sold eggs in the store as well. We had the best producing cows in the area. Everyone from the village would come and buy from us. We children helped cultivate the land. We were hard workers, eager to help with family chores. Six or seven Jewish families lived in Austzely, including my family and the other two Rothfeld brothers' families. Our neighbors were the families of Maurice Markowitz, the Friedman family, and the family of Emmanuel Weinberger. The rest of the families in Ausztley were non-Jews.

We didn't have enemies. We got along well with everyone. We went to non-Jewish weddings and burials. Like the Jews, most of the non-Jews were also farmers with vineyards and poultry. They stuffed the geese and took them to sell at the local market. During the grape harvest season, our non-Jewish neighbors brought us grapes for the holidays. We got along very well until the Germans came in.

I grew up surrounded by my first cousins, with all the excitement and pleasures that combining large families brings. My family led a modest existence, as my parents struggled to feed and clothe eight children. My father didn't have enough money to finish building our house. He spent all his earnings from the grocery store on the home and ran out of money when he got to the roof. To pay for the roof, he borrowed money from our neighbor Mr. Markowitz. One day, Mr. Markowitz came to my father and asked him to sign some papers. My father was suspicious but reluctantly signed them anyway.

We later learned that my father had signed over our land and our home to Mr. Markowitz. My father was devastated. My mother was in shock. My parents now had to pay Mr. Markowitz rent for the house and store. From then on, we suffered in poverty, from which we would never recover. For us girls, the hardest part was not having decent clothes to wear. We were in our late teens and early twenties, and our appearance was important to us. Occasionally, my sisters and I received a package of worn clothes from our mother's sister who lived in Philadelphia. My older sister Molvin was an experienced dressmaker, so she altered the dresses to suit us.

In Ausztely, we went to public school. Classes were taught in Hungarian, and the children had Russian lessons as part of the curriculum. Religious instruction was taught only to the Christian children. The Jewish children learned religion at home. My parents hired a teacher named Mr. Moher. He regularly came to our house to give us children private lessons in Jewish prayer and practice.

My family was Orthodox. At home, we were required to say our daily prayers, keep kosher, and strictly observe the Sabbath. At that time, it was traditional for only the men to go to synagogue. The women stayed home with the children and prepared the Sabbath meal. On the High Holy Days, the women joined the men for services, but the children were still excluded. It was not a real synagogue, but an uncle's large house used for prayer. The community did not have a rabbi or spiritual leader, so the local men conducted the services. If there was a bar mitzvah or other special occasion, they went to the synagogue in the nearby larger town of Beregszasz for the religious service.

My father took the Sabbath very seriously. No one was excluded. At sundown on Friday, the entire family was to be at home to celebrate together. Because the Sabbath laws were strictly enforced, we children were forbidden to even tear a piece of paper on the Sabbath. For the Shabbat meal, all eight of us children quietly sat around two tables as we attentively listened to our father pray. The four youngest children (Emil, Gizi, I, and Boreshka) sat at the smaller table. The four older children (Molvin, Reli, Miklosh, and Sanyi) sat with our parents at the more grown-up table. The whole family was very close, but I was especially close to my next oldest sister, Boreshka. She was a bright girl, always reading, and I admired her.

Had it not been for the war in Europe, the five of us daughters might never have married. The lack of family finances meant that we five daughters, already in our twenties, had nothing to offer but our good looks and kind hearts. It would have been difficult for us to marry.

My father was a kind and gentle man who adored his wife and family. In 1939, shortly after the heartache of losing our home, my father died of bone cancer. My mother and we eight siblings did the best we could with the abilities and resources we had. Molvin, the seamstress and dressmaker, brought in a little money to help the family exist. The three brothers helped manage the house, the store, and the land as best they could. I, the third youngest and twenty-one, was sent to a childless, older, married uncle to help in his home in Ujvar. He never went out of his way to do anything special for me. I did my job helping around the house as expected, cleaning, tending to him and his wife, and I didn't receive much more than room and board in return.

He was not nice to me. They had a lot of money, but he never bought me anything. Not even one single dress. However, one less mouth to feed at home was helpful to my family. I stayed there for a few years and then returned home after he died.

When I returned to Ausztely, the former Czech town was already occupied by the Hungarians. The days after I returned home were not like those before I left. It was 1944, and the Nazis were moving into Hungary very quickly.

Grandmother Ester Rothfeld (seated) and the four of her five daughters (Gizi missing) Boreshka, Molvin, Reli and Luizi

Grandfather David Rothfeld, late 1930s

Boreshka Rothfeld,
early 1940s

Emil Rothfeld, late
1930s to early 1940s

My family's first encounter with the Nazis came in the spring of 1944. At first, we were required to wear yellow stars on our clothes. Shortly after, the authorities came looking for my youngest brother Emil, who was eighteen. They said that they wanted him for work, but we hid him and pretended that he did not exist. A few weeks later, Emil, our neighbors the Mendelwitzes, and other local Jews were captured on the streets by the Hungarian SS. My mother and my younger sister, Gizi, went crying to the local Hungarian police known as the Csendor. They pleaded with the police to free Emil. The police knew my family well because they often trespassed through our property as a shortcut to a nearby village. They released Emil. We were ecstatic and relieved, but the excitement was short-lived.

One of our Christian neighbors heard about Emil's capture and offered to hide him, but Emil refused to go. Emil told our mother that he did not want to abandon the family. He told her that he knew he could face whatever was ahead of him, but he was worried about us girls. He wanted to stay with us. My two older brothers, Sanyi and Miklosh, had already moved out of our house. Miklosh was married and had a two-year-old girl named Livia.

Two weeks later, the "Shofed," or authorities, came. We watched, disbelieving, as the town's horse-drawn wagon carrying the local judge and the Csendor pulled up to our doorstep. We knew the judge. His name was Miklos Pak. He was one of our neighbors and not a very nice person. With a knock on the door, the nightmare began. It was the day after Passover. We were told to get ourselves together quickly. The authorities instructed my mother to relinquish all our family's gold and money as well as the key to the house. Our grocery store had long since been taken over by Christians. We were told to take a blanket, a change of clothes, and as much as we could carry on our backs.

Before leaving, Emil ran to the stall behind the house to say goodbye to the cows. When he returned to the wagon, he looked at the Csendor and asked that he please not lock the cat in the house. He was worried that the cat would be trapped while we were gone and not have food to eat. My four sisters, Emil, my mother, and I were placed on the wagon with our few belongings and taken on a half-hour journey to the local ghetto in Beregszasz. There was not a single Jewish person left in Ausztely.

The ghetto was an old brick factory in the center of town, guarded by the local Hungarian police. We didn't see any Germans but were informed by others that Beregszasz was a German headquarters. Upon our arrival, a pot was passed around, and we were given a final opportunity to hand over any gold or money that we had withheld. The authorities informed us that if anyone was found with any remaining gold or money, they would kill the children in front of the parents. We had little on us because we had handed most of our valuables over at the house. Petrified and threatened, my siblings and I threw in the rest: watches and jewelry we had hidden earlier in our clothing. The police said that they were keeping inventory of the confiscated items and that the items would go into a fund to aid those who were suffering in the war. Upon entering the ghetto, my mother was also forced to sign documents stating that the bonds she owned had been redeemed, but we never saw a single penny from those bonds.

We stayed in the ghetto for six weeks. At first, we ate the food we had carried with us from home. Some families had even brought kitchen equipment with them, so the women prepared food in the kitchen of the factory and distributed it first to the sick and then to the others. I was happy because my family was still together and because we had food to eat. I was with my mother and siblings. No one realized how dire our situation was.

Soon the food began to run out. The ground we slept on was solid concrete, cold and damp. We thought, or we tried to make ourselves believe, that we were waiting there for work. At least that was what they told us.

And then the transports started. The Hungarian police packed as many of the Jews from the ghetto into the trains as they possibly could. A few Jews were selected to assist with the journey. When those who assisted returned to transport the next group, they informed the others that the train was going all the way to Kassa, Hungary, and from there, the Jews were being handed over to the Germans.

My family was placed on the third transport. It was May 1944. My mother, Ester; my four sisters, Gizi, Molvin, Reli, Boreshka; and I, Luizi, all boarded the cattle cars. Emil had been taken earlier. The doors were locked, and darkness filled the car.

It felt there was no air in the train. We couldn't see out, and it was too dark to see much of anything inside. Except for Emil, we were still together. We had a little bit of food from the ghetto. The soldiers passed around a bucket for us to urinate and defecate in. There was no room to move. People sat on top of one another. When the train stopped and the doors were finally opened, we thought we were in Germany. We believed we had been brought there for work, but we were confused.

We were in Auschwitz, forced to stand in front of the German SS, and instructed to relinquish our remaining personal items as selections began. The SS looked us over, and with a simple point, we were sent to the right or to the left. Fortunately, we five sisters were still young and healthy despite the substandard conditions we had endured in the ghetto, so we still looked good. My four sisters and I were sent to the right as our dear mother was sent to the left. We knew it was not a good sign. She had been weeded out, and we could see the pattern. The elderly and those people with small children were being sent to the left, while those who were young and healthy were being sent to the right.

I'll never forget my mother in those minutes. I looked to where she stood on the other side, and I saw that she was gasping for air. I saw tears rolling down her cheeks as she desperately tried to hold them back. There was nothing she could say or do to help us or to help herself.

In Auschwitz, my youngest brother, Emil, who had been transported from the ghetto earlier, had the task of shoveling out the ashes from the crematorium. We later learned that on the day we arrived, Emil witnessed our mother going into the gas chamber.

The clothes we had brought with us were taken from us. We had to hand over everything that we had, and it was all thrown into a huge pile. All I had left was the dress on my body. We were taken inside to have our hair cut off. Our hair was cut so short that when we looked at one another, we were unrecognizable. We were told to strip and then sent to be disinfected. After that, we were thrown something to wear. The dress thrown at me was not mine, not the dress in which I had arrived.

My four sisters and I were taken to Lager C; *lager* is German for *barrack*. A few days after our arrival, Gizi ran into the lager with news she had overheard: we would soon be transferred to another, supposedly better lager; the people there did not seem to disappear as often as we had witnessed and heard about in our area.

The barrack next to us housed a Czechoslovakian Jewish family. They were envied by those in our barrack because the entire family was still together. One night, we heard the dogs barking and commotion coming from that Czech barrack. Everyone knew that when the dogs barked, no one was allowed to go outside. There was a great deal of noise and yelling, and suddenly everything was quiet. When we were finally allowed to go out, we realized that the Czech barrack was empty. The entire family was gone.

From Lager C, my sisters and I were taken to Lager B. There were twelve of us in Lager B, all Hungarian Jews. Aside from the twelve inmates, Rozsa was our Kapo, or supervisor. He was a Slovak who treated us decently. Those inmates who could speak German were assigned barrack chores that earned them better circumstances. They cleaned and neatened things up. They were the ones who rationed the food, so if there was a potato or something solid in the soup, they took it for themselves. Those Jews were not very nice. They allegedly washed their feet in the black coffee instead of giving it to us.

Soon after we arrived at Lager B, we were greeted by a male inmate. We were overjoyed by what he was saying. He came into our lager and told us that the younger children from the families were alive and that the mothers were taking care of them. With that news, we were optimistic that our mother might still be alive.

But despite the good news, he made it clear to us that we should take whatever opportunity to be transported out of Auschwitz. This message was meant to give us hope.

In Auschwitz, after weeks of limited food and hygiene, people began to get sick. The SS came around every day to look over the inmates. Those who did not look well were taken away.

We knew not to tell the soldiers if we were sick. We didn't know exactly what happened to those who got sick, but sometimes when the wind blew toward us, it brought burnt pieces of skin in the air. We smelled the burning skin smell. Later, we knew that when the crematorium could not handle everybody, the SS had a big lime pit that they put people in—dead or alive.

One day, the SS came to Lager B to select women for Bergen-Belsen. At this time, two of my sisters, Molvin and Gizi, were working in the leather factory in Auschwitz, so they were not in the barrack. After six weeks in Auschwitz, my two remaining sisters, Reli and Boreshka, and I were chosen to go to Bergen-Belsen. We boarded another freight car for our journey.

What I saw when I arrived at Bergen-Belsen, I will never forget. It was a mountain of shoes as high as a two-story house. They were the shoes of the people who had been exterminated. It was a real mountain of shoes.

Every morning at five, we were forced to line up outside. It was so cold. We stood there with our shaven heads and naked bodies for the selections. At that early morning hour, our fate was decided. To the right meant we were still fit to work; to the left, we died. It was that simple. We tried to look our best so that we might survive another day. If we could no longer produce, there was no need for us, and we were discarded.

Here, too, they checked the barracks for the sick. Those who were sick were taken away to a barrack known as "the hospital." It wasn't really a hospital. The people taken there just disappeared and were never seen again.

While we were in Bergen-Belsen we were each given a small amount of honey on rare occasions, and I'm not sure why. It was so good. But otherwise, the food was grassy broth and a piece of bread for breakfast, no lunch, and a cup of black coffee for dinner. We were hungry. Some people could not resist and ate their piece of bread all at once. Others tried to nibble on the small piece, crumb by crumb, so that it would last the whole day.

One day when we were in the lager, I noticed a young girl of about seventeen lying across from me. She was desperately staring at me as I nibbled at my bread. She was so frail looking. I could see that she was very, very hungry. We were all starving, but some of us tolerated the hunger better than others. I couldn't bear to watch her suffering, so I gave her a piece of my bread. I couldn't have enjoyed it knowing how badly she wanted it.

Occasionally, we were given a little water with which

to wash. There was nothing to do but lie in our bunks, crammed together. We were packed so tightly in the wooden bunks that if one of us shifted, we all had to shift. Fortunately, we were not in Bergen-Belsen for too long before some manufacturers from Magdeburg, Germany, came to select those of us fit for work. We were made to march in front of them as they looked us over and selected those of us they deemed able to work. We sisters were still holding up, still able to appear capable of work. We had the remains of our strength from home, from the country. We still had a bit of color in our cheeks and looked generally healthy, so all three of us were chosen.

In December 1944, Reli, Boreshka, and I boarded a train for a 137-kilometer trip from Bergen-Belsen to Magdeburg, Germany, on the western bank of the Elbe River. We arrived at the partially bombed-out Polta factory. In the morning, we were given wooden shoes to wear. We had to march to the factory every day in those very uncomfortable shoes. One week we worked from six o'clock in the morning until six o'clock in the evening and the next week from six o'clock in the evening until six o'clock in the morning. As we marched to the factory in the morning, we walked past the group of inmates who had been working the night shift. We could see their anguish. Their faces had a greenish hue from exhaustion. Those of us who arrived in the morning looked a little better after a few hours of sleep.

We sisters worked in a makeshift ammunition factory and were stationed in the part of the factory undamaged by previous bombings. The night shift was particularly hard to tolerate. We worked for twelve hours without food. Sometimes, I felt so tired that I struggled desperately to keep my eyes open, especially around two or three in the morning. In the factory, we were guarded by a Lithuanian woman and a German guard. One night, an older German mechanic was assigned to guard us for the night. It was the middle of the night, and I could see that he was watching me as I struggled to stay awake. He walked toward me. I was so frightened of what he would say or do that I sat trembling in fear. To my surprise, he asked me if I wanted to lie down in the boiler room for a few minutes. I thanked him and just put my head on the table for a few minutes to rest. I was so grateful. If the guards were pleased with our work in the factory, we were rewarded with a teaspoon of mustard. It only made us hungrier.

We were told that for Christmas we would receive extra food. We were excited and looked forward to it, but the food never came. Instead, the SS men who watched over us received Christmas packages from their families and made us carry their packages as they walked next to us empty-handed. I could tell that the SS men were from Hanover because of the addresses on the packages.

We worked very hard in Magdeburg. They didn't let us rest one single day, not even on Sunday when they made us carry large rocks back and forth in the factory courtyard. It was winter with snow and ice everywhere. They made us carry stones from one place to another and then all the way back again. They made us carry them just so we couldn't rest.

By now, my older sister, Reli, was wearing down, losing her strength and her ability to work well. She had constant diarrhea that had started before we left Bergen-Belsen. She was very weak but continued to work because the alternative, known as "the hospital," was not to be considered.

One day when we were in our barracks, the Magdeburg factory was bombed. The Polish girls broke out of the barracks, and the rest of us inmates followed them down to the bunker for safety. But the German soldiers came looking for us and forced us out.

They shot at us as we ran in every direction, and then they seemed to disappear. I felt so weak and tired, so I wandered back to the barracks and fell asleep. When I woke up, it was raining and very, very cold. As I tried to move, I realized that I was lying in a puddle and that the entire side of my body was numb. It took over an hour before the numbness disappeared and I could find the strength to get up.

I wandered around until I found my sisters. We believed that the Germans had fled soon after the bombing. My sisters and I, along with others, went into the officers' kitchen in search of food. The Germans used

French chefs, and the food that was cooked for them was excellent. We were so happy. We had food, good food, and we thought the nightmare was over. But the next morning came the Wehrmacht, or German army. These defensive forces gathered us together and marched us on foot to the bank of a lake. We could see a horse racing track nearby, and behind that were buildings where we believed the German soldiers were housed.

The Russian army was advancing, and the Germans knew it was time to flee. During construction of the concentration camps, the Nazis had buried explosive mines around the perimeters to prevent inmates from escaping. Now the SS were trying to escape, and they used the remaining survivors to help them cross the minefields.

It was April 13, 1945. My sisters Reli and Boreshka and I were forced to walk through the minefields. If we stopped for a few seconds, the SS shot at us as they yelled *"Raus, Raus!"* I can still see their angry, heartless faces and the coldness in their eyes.

We were together, Boreshka and Reli and I, but Boreshka was having trouble walking and couldn't keep up. She had a fever and a large red bump with ulcers on her leg; in Hungarian we called this disease Orbans. The German SS put her on the wagon and told us to march onward. We didn't want to, but we did as we were told.

We were terrified that something would happen to her, but we had no choice. If we didn't continue as instructed, they would fire at us. After a few minutes, we looked back. Boreshka and the wagon had disappeared. We panicked. There was no time to think, but we had to act fast as the Nazis forced us onward. Soon, Reli and I approached a fork in the road, and we didn't know which way to go. I told Reli that I thought that the wagon with Boreshka would most likely take one path, but Reli felt strongly that it would be the other. We were confused and frightened about making the wrong decision and losing her. We had no time to decide, and as we stood frozen in fear, the approaching SS shot at us to keep us moving. We did move, but it turned out to be the wrong path.

Soon after, the city of Magdeburg got an ultimatum, and the SS feared for their lives. Because of the escaping SS near Ravesbavok, we knew that the Russians were very close by. As the Russian soldiers got closer, the SS troops panicked and left, leaving us alone.

Reli and I and two other girls who were with us from Beregszasz began to walk, though we had no idea where we were going. We found a barn in a town called Malhov (Malaav). Inside, we found a pile of hay, and we were so exhausted that we lay down and slept. During the night, we awoke to Germans speaking outside the barn: "Go this way! Go that way!" We heard traffic and noise, then quiet. All night, we listened to silence.

In the morning, Russian soldiers came into the barn. They asked us if Germans were around; we now knew that the voices we had heard during the night were those of SS soldiers fleeing from the Russians.

When the Russian soldiers approached us, we were in shock, not believing our eyes. We slowly understood that there was a good chance that we had survived. Even though we knew that the Russians were rescuing us, we were afraid of them. We had heard through the grapevine that they raped young female survivors, and we were afraid that they might rape us, too. It was May 8, 1945. Reli and I believed that everything was over and that we would go home to find Boreshka already there.

Everyone wanted to go home. Survivors wandered the streets looking for family, food, shelter, and transportation home. We walked and walked, trying to figure out how to get home. We came to a forest where we saw a few Russian soldiers with prisoners. We didn't go near them because we were still afraid of them.

We encountered a group of Jewish men who came up to us and spoke to us in Hungarian. They asked us if we had seen their wives. We had not. People wandered all over, asking others if they had seen friends or family. We asked the men if they could help us find a place to sleep for the night. They took us to the building where they had been staying. They were good to us and brought us food to eat. They let us stay in that building and left to find themselves another place. We stayed for a few days, sleeping and eating, getting our strength back, and trying to figure out what to do next. Russian soldiers brought us bread to eat, and we were grateful. We were now less afraid of them and realized that they had saved our lives. We searched everywhere for food. We even searched empty apartments and found a few rags that we could use for clothes.

For the next few months, Reli and I and the two other women stayed in various homes along the way, waiting for our turn to be transported back home. We were told by humanitarian organizations that soon all Czechs and Hungarians from Subcarpathia would be transported home. That was where our home was. But there were thousands of Hungarians and Czechs waiting for transport. We knew it would not be easy. We stayed until December 1945. We decided not to wait any longer for the promised transport and instead to try to get home any way we could. It had been seven months since our liberation.

One of the girls with us spoke Russian, and she was able to communicate with Russian soldiers along the way. As we walked, we came across people we knew. We asked them if they had seen Boreshka. They told us that they had seen her in what were most likely her final days.

They said, "Your sister was sick and all alone. How could you have left her?"

I was devastated. Those words have haunted me ever since.

In total, my mother, Ester, age 54; two of my brothers, Sanyi, 39, and Emil, 19; and my sister, Boreshka, 34, were killed by the Nazis. Five of my siblings survived, including my brother Miklosh, 35, whose wife and two-year-old daughter named Livia were killed in Auschwitz, and four sisters: Reli, 32, Molvin, 28, me, Luiza, 26 and Gizi, 25. Of the forty-two members of my family, only twelve survived the concentration camps.

When Reli and I finally arrived home in Ausztely, a Christian family was living in our house. A pig rooted in the dirt of our yard. One of our cows grazed across the street with the nasty judge, Miklos Pak, who had rounded us up eighteen months earlier for the ghetto. The judge told my brother that the cow did not produce any milk while we were away, so he wanted my brother to pay him for keeping the cow. My brother lost both the cow and the money. Everything was gone. They took the cows, the farm machinery, and all the tools. Everything was taken from us, and we got nothing back. While we were gone, the villagers had taken whatever they wanted, and when we returned, no one was eager to give anything back.

I stayed in Ausztely for a few days with a Jewish neighbor. The kind Christian neighbors, who had originally tried to save my younger brother, Emil, brought us flour and food. The other old neighbors mostly avoided us. They were uneasy around us, not knowing how to face our return or not wanting to hear what we had experienced.

I left Ausztely to stay with my only surviving brother, Miklosh. He was living in Matéfalva, Hungary. I decided that I wanted to leave Hungary altogether, so I joined the Hagsharah, a Zionist organization that helped prepare young Jewish pioneers for their journey to Palestine. The women washed and cleaned, while the men worked in the fields. No one worked very hard. I arrived at the Hagsharah toward the end of the operation, so most of the adults had already been transported. Most of those left with me were children between the ages of eight and ten.

I stayed there for six weeks. I thought about going to relatives in America via Italy, but one night about one hundred of us from the Hagsharah were instructed to go outside and board a truck. We were taken from Hungary to Yugoslavia. We waited in Yugoslavia with the Hagsharah with the plan of reaching *Eretz Yisrael* (the Land of Israel). We were told that we would soon be taken by ship to Palestine via the Haganah, or the Jewish underground. We waited, knowing it could be only a moment's notice before we were to leave for our new homeland. We were taught a Hebrew Passover Seder song and were instructed to immediately speak words from the song as we passed border patrols. We were to do this so that the border police would believe we were speaking Hebrew and returning home to Palestine. The border patrols were also paid for their silence.

The next day, we were secretly taken by train to board a ship named the *Rafiah* (previously named the *Athina*) in Bakar, Yugoslavia, filled with some 800 refugees who had dreams of a new beginning in the Zionist state. Commandeered by six agents of the Israeli Mossad, the ship departed from Yugoslavia on November 26, 1946, for a twelve-day journey in the Ionian Sea.

On December 7, 1946, after an eleven-day journey, the ship arrived off Sirna Island. The ship was to meet another boat, which never arrived. As we waited, a storm approached, and the captain decided to enter a large bay that was not well protected. While attempting to anchor, the ship ran aground and began to take on water.

We had no choice but to jump and swim ashore, or we would go down with the ship. The men went first. They tied ropes to the ship and then swam ashore. We were instructed to jump as the wind blew the boat closer to shore. A few of us jumped at a time. We were able to pull ourselves to shore with the ropes and the help of the men. I remember a group of Romanian girls on the boat who were seasick. Unfortunately, they were not able to regain their strength, and they went down with the ship. I particularly remember an obese woman who would not let go of her pocketbook. After much persuading from the crew and passengers, she reluctantly jumped with the pocketbook in hand. She struggled in vain to hold on to the rope but could not. We all watched in horror as she went under in the rough seas, still clutching her bag. In all, eight people drowned.

At first, there was nothing to eat but snails. Some people ate them, but I couldn't. By this time, the British

knew an illegal boat had disappeared, so they were
searching for us. The next day, the British ship HMS
Providence, the destroyer HMS *Chevron*, and the Greek
warships HMS *Themistocles* and HMS *Aegean* set out to
rescue us survivors. We were taken to a detention camp
in Cyprus.

At the detention camp, I met people I knew who were
on the *Knesset Israel*, the ship that had left Yugoslavia
right before the *Rafiah*. I was ecstatic to find my first
cousins and neighbors from Ausztely, Mendi and Uli
Rothfeld. They had arrived a few days earlier on the
Bracha Fold, which had embarked on October 22, 1946,
right before the *Knesset*.

I stayed at the detention camp in Cypress for about
six weeks. We were allowed priority entrance into
Palestine because our ship had sunk. I was taken to
Kiryat Shmuel, near Haifa, where I stayed in quarantine
for six more weeks. The conditions there were not too
bad. We lived in tents made of fabric. We had food, good
conversation, and the opportunity to make new friends.

On May 19, 1947, on the authority of the Palestinian
government, I was officially released from the Kiryat
Shmuel Detention Camp as an immigrant of Palestine.
Because I had no family in Palestine, I was placed in a
girls' home in Petah Tikva, near Tel Aviv, slightly more
than five months from the start of my voyage from
Yugoslavia.

The Rafiah, 1946

My mother at the girl's home (Beth Hechaluzoth Spiera) Petah Tikva, Israel, 1947(second to last row, sixth from left)

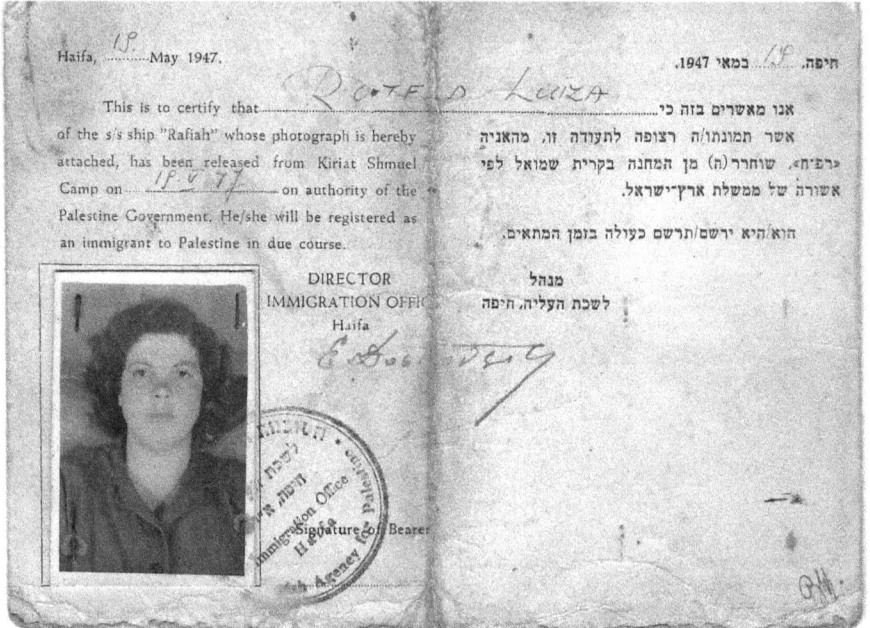

My mother's entry papers into Palestine, 1947

MY FATHER

My father was an enigma. On rare occasions, he revealed trivial bits of information about his life. I knew very little about him and almost nothing about his family. He was a disassociated member of our household who had severed all ties with his family's few remaining survivors. We knew little about him, and he cared to know little about us. He was a reclusive stranger living in our home.

When I was already an adult with my own children, my father reluctantly began to tell me some of his wartime stories. He was a wonderful storyteller, but he rarely spoke of his wartime experience and almost never spoke about his family. My father's way of telling his story was full of fragments, full of missing pieces. I desperately wanted to know something about him, as I felt I hardly knew him. I was hungry for information about him and his family. It appeared to me that he had no connections, or so he led me to believe. He was a blank slate. We accepted who he was because there wasn't much we could do about it. He lived beside us, not with us. Most of the family avoided him, and he avoided them. I was his main contact and the voice between him and all the other members of our family. Here is his narrative in his voice.

⧜⧜

My father, Moishe, was one of eleven children, seven girls (Piroshka, Hoinalka, Molvin, Rivka, Shari, Bela, and Rochel) and four boys (Moishe, Villi, Armin, and Jeno). My grandfather, Leon (Lieb) Hofstadter, was a famous cantor who frequented the United States. He was a good friend to the famous American cantor Yosele Rosenblatt. They met before Yosele emigrated from Hungary and became "big" in America.

My grandfather, Lieb, decided to follow in Yosele's footsteps and went to America to make his fortune. His first stop was to see Yosele, who gave him a personal letter of introduction. It was the early 1920s, and with that letter, my grandfather was accepted everywhere and was able to get jobs as a cantor. Grandfather Lieb was much sought after in America, especially on the High Holy Days. In a short time, my grandfather made a lot of money. He was the life of every party. His voice was amazing. The walls shattered as he sang. At weddings, people pushed him to get up on the table to sing and dance.

In 1920s America, Grandfather Lieb was disappointed with the Jewish religious way of life, so he returned to

Hungary with ten thousand dollars of his earnings. Before leaving America, he learned how to make matzo by machine and purchased equipment to start a matzo and wine factory in Hungary.

Grandfather Lieb was born in Dukla, Poland, which was on the Polish–Hungarian border. Because of this, he was able to get Hungarian citizenship. But it only applied to him and any of his children under the age of eighteen, so it didn't help the rest of our family during World War II. Initially, his citizenship papers helped him, but soon the Hungarian government declared all Jews in Hungary as persons "without a homeland." My mother, Marie Altman, had three sisters, Ilonka, Aranka, and Lily and three brothers Laci, Andor, and Bala. Uncle Andor owned a successful lumberyard in Poroszllo, Hungary, and he supported my mother and all of his other sisters and brothers.

Grandfather Lieb had a brother named Chaim Hirsh Hofstadter. He had sixteen children with three wives and lived in Pressburg, Hungary (now called Bratislava, Slovakia). In 1938, one of his daughters married a cantor named Stern from Manchester, England. The cantor was able to bring Chaim and his entire family over to England, and in that way, he saved them all from the Nazis.

During my childhood, my father managed a farm in Kishkunhalas, Hungary, where we lived, approximately 134 kilometers south of Budapest. In 1927, when I was nine, my father lost part of his eyesight to glaucoma. With limited access to medical treatment, he changed his work and, like his father, Lieb, became a cantor and a *shochet* (kosher slaughterer) for a synagogue in a small town outside of Budapest called Nagyteteni. The family moved into a small house at 5 Iskola Utca, which was a few doors down from the synagogue. I was sent to study away from home in the cheyder, which is a Jewish school. I ate meals with local Jewish families and lived with many different relatives.

Upon finishing my studies at the cheyder, I attended the Nyilvanos and Polgaris Escola in Budapest, and I was an excellent student with an insatiable desire for knowledge. I went on to study at the teachers college in Budapest, but when the war started, it became clear that I would not be able to teach as a Jew, so I studied the Torah for the next three and a half years at the Yeshiva in Paks, which was approximately one hundred kilometers from Budapest.

Despite Grandfather Lieb's good fortune and frequent visits to the United States, he was unable to help my family leave Hungary and escape the Nazis. My father was captured in 1944, soon after the Nazi occupation of Hungary, when he was traveling by train and the police asked to see his identification. He didn't have the proper ID, so they took him to a kind of Hungarian concentration camp called Kistarcsa. From there, he was most likely taken to Auschwitz because we never heard from him again.

At the age of twenty-three, I was drafted into the Hungarian army's forced labor unit. My unit was placed in the Nagyteteni Castle, a few blocks from our home. During the day, we were taken to the mountain area to break huge boulders into smaller rocks to be used for building material. At night, we slept on the top floor of the castle. After I had experienced a few months of forced labor, a new Minister of the Hungarian army was in place. He was respectful of the Jewish soldiers and ordered that we be put back into military duty and, like all the other soldiers, be given weapons. Our equality lasted eight months, after which we were again stripped of our weapons and returned to forced labor units.

A few months after being in forced labor, I was able to obtain Christian papers from the Swiss embassy, and I had taken on the name Laszlo Holossy. I took the last name Holossy from one of our neighbors, a nice old lady who lived in Nagyteteni. I left the forced labor unit and stayed in a safe house in Budapest under the protection of the Swiss embassy. One day, the safe house was raided by the Arrow Cross, also known as the Hungarian Nazis, and we were all captured. It was October 1944. I was twenty-five years old. I was one of thousands captured by the Germans, one of thousands transported by cattle car to the concentration camps. We were packed in like a bunch of sardines, cold and hungry, and each moment wondering where our fate would lead us. As I looked around the train, I noticed a window. It was a small one, smaller than you could imagine, but I knew that it was my only chance. I suddenly remembered that as a small child, I had read a book that said if your head fit through an opening, the rest of your body will also fit. At that moment, I felt the urge to say a little prayer. Although, as you can imagine, I was bitter about religion, faith, hope, and God himself, I said the prayer anyway. I saw someone else squeeze through the window, and I followed him. Huge electrical poles stood approximately every ten or twelve yards. It was the dead of night, and the train rushed along so quickly. I knew that if I jumped at the wrong second, I would hit one of the poles and surely die. But the alternative was to be killed just as certainly. Miraculously, I survived the jump.

As I got up from the fall, I looked around. Not quite sure where I was, I only knew that we had been on our way to Austria. We were about ten kilometers from the Austrian border, and I knew that this would be my last chance. We were told that the train would take us to Hegyeshalom, Hungary, on the Austrian border, but what would happen from there I could only imagine. We had heard about the concentration camps and crematoriums, so I was terrified. The train was just about to cross the border, and from there, it would be the camps. I began to think about my family. Where were they? Would I ever see them again? The last time I saw my mother was when I was ordered to enlist in the Hungarian army. She came with me to the gate. I kissed her and said goodbye. I never saw her again.

I couldn't think about it. I had to move on. Looking around, I saw that I was alone in a field, surrounded by piles of hay. I opened a pile of hay and buried myself in the center. It seemed like a good place to hide for the night. After a short while, I began to get restless and decided to leave. As I walked, I reached into my pocket and found a packet of raw tobacco. I looked around for some raw husk and rolled myself a cigarette. Suddenly, I noticed a road ahead of me. As I got closer, I saw army trucks and German soldiers. If they were to see me with my torn clothes, unshaven, and filthy, I knew that they would capture me immediately. I walked a little closer and saw a bridge. I moved so close that it became impossible for me to turn back. A soldier patrolled the bridge, a tough-looking guy who paced back and forth with a rifle in hand. I thought to myself, *Now, what do I do?*

My instincts took over. I started to whistle a tune. With my cigarette in hand and confidence on my face, I walked in front of the soldier and over the bridge. I walked into the village and stopped at a pub. It was full of German soldiers, drinking and laughing. I was so hungry! I thought to myself, *I don't care if I drop dead or if someone kills me, but I must find something to eat.* I walked some more and came to a village house with a light on. I knocked on the door. A peasant woman opened it. Again, my instincts took over.

"Good evening," I said. "My family and I have been evacuated from our home because of bombings. I'm a little hungry and was wondering if you might have something to eat."

I can assure you that she did not believe a word I was saying.

Suddenly, a young man came to the door. He was a tall boy, around nineteen, and somewhat friendly like his mother. The two of them stood in the doorway looking me over.

Finally, the woman said, "OK, come on in and sit down. I'll get you something to eat."

I was convinced that she was leaving the room to alert the police, but I had made peace with my fate. To my surprise, she came back to the table with a loaf of bread and a container of milk in her hand. I was so hungry that I could hardly wait for her to cut the bread. I wanted to grab it with my bare hands, but I knew that this would make her suspicious—if she wasn't already. She cut the bread and served me a slice. Her son came back into the kitchen. He sat down next to me and started to talk. He said that he worked there on the farm but that his real ambition was to learn a trade and go to work in the city.

Because he was a country boy and appeared eager to listen, I told him that I had worked as a machinist and that if he were to come to the city one day, I might be able to help him out. He was delighted to hear this. The woman returned, this time carrying a bag full of food.

"Here, take this," she said with a warm smile.

She instructed me that it was time to go, and she

directed me to the railroad station. I knew that it was time for me to move on.

I mentioned that it seemed to me that I was about five kilometers from the army hospital where I had been hospitalized about a year before with a bladder infection. Most of the men at the hospital were being treated for venereal diseases. My best friend at the hospital was Levi Weiss. We were like brothers. I decided that I would try to reach the hospital before dark. I was optimistic that some of my old friends would still be there to help me out. The peasant woman, obviously knowing who I really was, warned me to be careful because there were many police surrounding the railroad station. I thanked the mother and son and left.

As I reached the railroad station, I saw it for myself. The woman was right. I was too frightened to go into the station, so I kept walking. I walked for two and a half hours until I reached the city of Győr, where the hospital was. There on the front steps stood a soldier, an old Hungarian peasant, guarding the entranceway. As if someone were holding my hand, I walked toward the guard and smiled as I passed him. He recognized me and let me in. When I walked inside, I was delighted to see that my Hungarian soldier buddies were still there. They could tell exactly where I had been and where I had been destined. They didn't say much, but I could see that they were worried. I spent a few hours with them. They collected a little money for me, and I left for the railroad station in Győr once more.

It was near the end of 1944. At the railroad station, I saw another guy about my age, and I don't think that he was Jewish. I also didn't look too Jewish myself because I have blue eyes and light hair. When the train came, we boarded together. He invited me to sit near him. He took out a package with some bread and bacon and invited me to have some with him. When we got to Budapest, he warned me to be careful at the exits. I was fortunate to get out of the station without being noticed. I wanted to take the trolley to the center of Budapest, but instead I walked on the street.

Someone came up behind me, noticed I had a full beard and lice, and whispered in my ear, "Go to the barber right away."

I returned to the Swiss embassy, and they sent me to the army hospital, which was in the basement of the local movie theater. I was put to work assisting in the operating room. One morning as I was looking out the window, I saw that there were Russian soldiers walking around outside. They had invaded Budapest, and the war was over.

In the end, the entire Jewish population of Nagyteteni was gone except for one Jewish woman, Magda Blier. She was married to a Christian man, Ferenz Hilko, who had hidden her in the closet. I lost my entire family in Auschwitz: my mother, Marie, age 48; my father, Moishe, 53; and my only brother, Stephan, 21. Stephan was four years younger than me.

With no family and nowhere to go, I went to the office of the United Nations Relief and Rehabilitation Agency (UNRRA) in Budapest. It was the central office for Hungarian Jews, and at the time, they assisted refugees who wanted to immigrate to Palestine. I told them I wanted to go to Palestine. A Lithuanian man from the Haganah entered the office and walked over to me. He looked me up and down and said that he thought they could possibly use me for a Zionist mission. He spoke only vaguely of what the mission would be. What I knew for sure was that the goal was to reach Palestine.

I was soon told that a group of thirty Jewish Holocaust survivors from Hungary expected to begin an illegal journey to Palestine. I was elected to be their leader. The plan was for us to get to Yugoslavia and from Yugoslavia, to Italy. Our final destination was to be Kibbutz Ma'anit, near Haifa. Within a few days, I met the group as we gathered for the beginning of our excursion. We headed for the central railroad station in Budapest and boarded a train for Yugoslavia.

The train stopped in Zagreb. We didn't have documents, but no one seemed to care. The borders were open, and Europe was in a state of chaos, so our lack of travel documents was easily overlooked. We were told at the Zionist headquarters not to speak Hungarian, only Hebrew. The only Hebrew we knew was from prayers, so we repeated those words in Hebrew gibberish.

In Yugoslavia, another official from the Zionist organization informed us that we would be going to

Trieste, Italy. It was January 1946. When we arrived in Trieste, a young man with a horse and buggy was waiting to take us to the Zionist organization on Via De Mila Seta. Hungry and tired from our long journey, we arrived and were given our first gift: a few cans of food and an orange. We ate the oranges, skins and all.

The next day, we were told to go to the railroad station and board a train to Rome. From Rome, we continued on to the Po Valley in Milan to the Grotta Ferata. The Grotta Ferata was a beautiful palace formerly inhabited by the Italian fascists. It was now empty and being used by the Zionist organization. When we walked in, we were greeted by a physician. He placed his stethoscope on my chest.

"How old are you?" he asked.

"Twenty–five," I answered.

He turned to me and said, "Your heart sounds like that of an eighty-year-old man."

I was so exhausted that I wasn't surprised.

We were introduced to two wonderful women, one Italian and one Polish. The Italian woman was Eva Pitoni. The Polish woman's name I don't recall. They were employed by the Zionist organization to look after us. They cooked and cared for us until we were ready for the next leg of our journey. The women handed each of us a pair of new pajamas and a robe and instructed us to take a bath. Afterward, we were led to large, shared bedrooms. One of the members of our group was a great storyteller, and we listened to him for hours until we fell asleep from fatigue.

The next morning, I was still very tired. The physician suggested that I be transported to a sanatorium near Rome, where I could rest and regain my strength. I was taken to Santa Maria De Roma where I was closely cared for and well fed. After ten days, I returned to the palace with my health renewed. No one recognized me because I had gained a lot of weight in that short time.

A few days after my return, two soldiers from the Jewish unit of the Royal Army Service Corps (RASC) came in and announced to our group that they were in need of someone for a "special assignment." From the group of thirty, ten of us were selected to be interviewed. I was among the ten. One by one, we went into a private room to be questioned. I was the last in line. I closed the door, and the two soldiers studied me carefully. I stood terrified, uncertain of what they wanted.

Finally, one of the soldiers asked, "Do you speak Hebrew?"

Relieved, I answered, "No."

"Can you count to ten in Hebrew?"

"Yes," I said.

"Let me hear," he said.

So I started, "*Echad, shtaim, shalosh….*"

"Very good, very good," he said. "You speak Hebrew. You will be perfect."

What I would be perfect for, I didn't know. But whatever it was, I didn't think I could handle it.

"I don't feel very good," I said.

"What's wrong?" asked the soldier.

"My heart!"

He turned to me and said, "What you have to do has nothing to do with your heart."

I later learned that I was chosen, for one simple reason: I did not have a number tattoo from the concentration camps, and that was perfect camouflage for the assignment.

The next morning, in preparation for my assignment, I said goodbye to my group. We hoped to see one another again in Palestine. Two of our group members were shoemakers, and they gave me a pair of shoes. I was to leave with the two soldiers the following morning for my secret mission. We went to Caserta, near Naples, for military training, where I handed over my clothes in exchange for a British Royal Army Service Corps uniform—and a tommy gun.

"From now on, you are Shlomo Weinstock," one of the RASC soldiers said.

Shlomo Weinstock was a Jewish soldier from Kfar Varburg, Palestine. I was given his identity for my mission to Palestine. He, in turn, would take on my identity and stay in Italy, organizing the illegal immigration of Jewish Holocaust survivors to Palestine with the Zionist organization. I was to become Shlomo Weinstock from Kfar Varburg, near Gidera.

On the first day, a sergeant arrived and gave the four of us new arrivals a speech: "You have a few weeks to learn what others learn in two years. You will now begin your training."

That day, we started our drills with the tommy guns. Two weeks later, we packed our things, got ready to leave, boarded the military truck waiting outside, and were taken to a transit camp in Naples. The next day, we were taken by truck again to the Naples harbor, where a 35,000-ton ship awaited us. The ship had been comandeered from the Japanese. I boarded the troop ship with the three other men, two of them Polish and the third Lithuanian. Within three days, we arrived in Port Said, Egypt, where we were taken to the desert military camp Quasasin (Casasen). The British army had some 100,000 soldiers at this camp. It was the middle of the desert, and most of the workers were German POWs. The British soldiers didn't want to help us move into Palestine; they felt that they had helped us enough, and the rest was for us to figure out.

The next morning, the officers met to discuss our situation. We two or three hundred men felt there was only one language that the British would understand: hunger strike. We refused to eat for a day or two. Then word came that a truck would soon be coming for us. We boarded the truck and then a cattle car at the railroad station. We soon spotted the Suez Canal and could see large passenger ships, along with transport ships, passing both ways through the canal. I was more tired than excited, so I closed my eyes and fell asleep.

I slept until I was awakened by the morning light. I looked out the train window and saw bunkers all around and soldiers with guns.

"Where are we?" I asked aloud.

"We are in Palestine," someone on the train answered.

The train pulled into the railroad station in Rehovot, and we were taken to a discharge camp run by the British army. Before leaving the train, I was handed a suit, shoes, and a few other items of clothing. I remained in Rehovot for two weeks and was then sent to Kibbutz Vav in Rishon Letzion with another Jewish organization, HaShomer Hatzier, where I stayed for another two weeks. I was finally given a pass so that I could return to the discharge camp to be officially discharged from the Royal Army Service Corps, as Shlomo Weinstock.

After the discharge, I returned to Kibbutz Vav, but I was very anxious to get back to my original group from Italy. An officer from the Haganah came to me and asked me to hand over all the salary that I had been paid as Shlomo Weinstock. After all, it was his salary, not mine. It was now very difficult for me to find the others because I didn't have money for travel. I went to the office at the Sachnut, telling them that I wanted to find my group at Kibbutz Ma'anit in Karpes Pardes, near Haifa. In Italy, we had made a plan to reconnect there. At the office, they gave me money to take the bus to the kibbutz.

When I arrived, I was thrilled to see the entire group still alive. They told me they were envious that I had been able to leave; their journey had been very difficult. They were put on an old wrecked ship, and on the way to Palestine, they were intercepted mid-ocean by the

British army and, like most other illegal Jewish ships, taken to Cyprus. It was a very rough journey, and they were fortunate to have survived once again. I stayed at Kibbutz Ma'anit for a year and a half. From there, I went to Kibbutz Ritzon Litcon.

I wanted to leave the kibbutz, but I didn't have money, so it was not possible. Some of the kibbutz members were originally from Bratislava, Czechoslovakia. One day, a man came to me and said that his mother was a Hofstadter. We wondered if we were related. Then one day, his brother, Yossi, came to visit from England, and we discovered that he had connections to my grandfather's brother, Chaim Hirsch Hofstadter, who had immigrated to England—as I mentioned before—in 1938 when his daughter married a cantor from England. He managed to get me Chaim Hirsch's address. I wrote him a letter in Hebrew, and one of my friends translated it into Yiddish. In the letter, I asked Chaim for the addresses of my aunts and uncles in America and Canada.

Within a few weeks, he sent me a letter with the addresses. I wrote to my Aunt Molvin, my father's oldest sister, in Cleveland, and within a short time, I received a letter saying how happy she was to hear from me and that from my picture, I looked like Uncle Jeno, my father's brother. She was sorry that because their financial situation was not too good, she could not send more than the ten dollars she'd enclosed. But ten dollars was enough for me to leave the kibbutz, as I'd planned.

Shortly thereafter, I was recruited to join the Palmach, the underground Jewish military, as a machinist. I was placed in Halon, in the Betharoshet Michsav, a silver cutlery factory. There the Palmach was given space to build weapons to prepare for military operations. We worked from a large empty container. We set up a technical unit and were given permission to go into the factory to use the machines as needed. There we built hundreds of rockets and rocket launchers to be used by the Palmach. It was 1947, and the Palmach was trying to take over Faluja, Egypt.

Until this point, the Palmach had not been successful in taking over Faluja, which was on the border with Egypt. We built a small tank about three feet long and loaded it with bombs. We were able to activate the bombs from the top of our building via remote control, and with this device, we captured the town. The engineer who designed the device was named Halpern. He was from Romania.

Later, we set up shop in an Arab village, where we occupied a few homes. We brought in machinery to fabricate metal parts, and I worked on the electrical components of the little tank. We also built hundreds of rockets. We built booby traps. My leaders were Yigal Alon and Yitzhak Sadeh. After the declaration of the State of Israel, the Palmach was dismantled, and I joined the Israeli army.

The Hofstadter's- Jeno, Moshe (my grandfather) Lieb (my great grandfather), Villi and Armin.

My Great Grandparents Lieb and Leah Hofstadter

The Hofstadter's (L to R) Rochel, Leah
(my great grandmother) Ilonka and her daughter's.

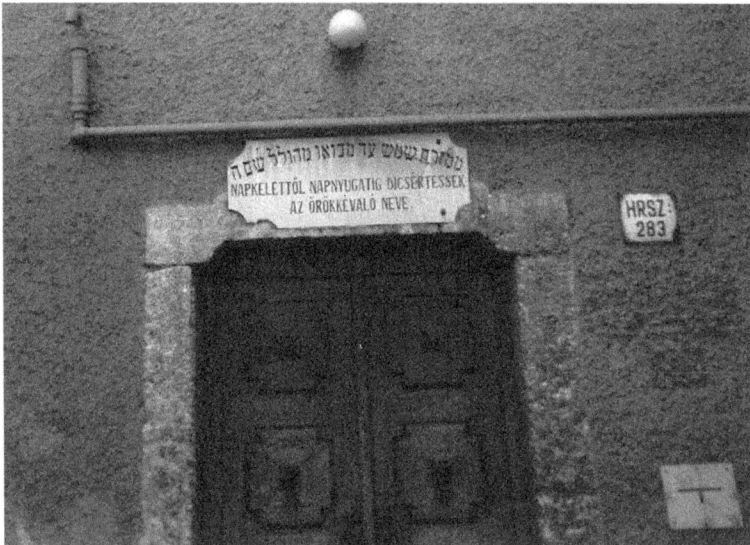

Grandfather Moshe's synagogue in Nagyteteni, 2009

Altman Family (left to right) Elona, Marie (my grandmother), Ethel (my great grandmother), Aranka and her two children, cousin Rubinstein and Lily.

Altman Family (left to right) Rubenstein and wife Lily with their child, Ethel (my grandmother) Bela and Helen with their two children, Elona

My father (second row seated, second from left) with the group he led to Italy-Kibbutz Ma anit, Palestine-1947

My Father's Palmach Document-Palestine, 1947

THE EARLY YEARS
ISRAEL

While at the home for girls in Petah Tikva, my mother, Luizi worked in an aluminum factory, molding sheet metal into lanterns. In her final months there, she also worked as a housekeeper. She was given a small room to share with four other young women. One of them, Ibby Hartman, became her best friend and would later go to Kibbutz Naharia with her. After Cyprus and the lack of stability that she had experienced for those last several years, my mother felt this to be a home and a form of family. It was where my mother celebrated the inception of the State of Israel. Her goal was to make enough money to leave, marry, and have a home of her own.

My parents' first cousins were married to each other. Moti was my father's first cousin, and she was married to my mother's first cousin, Sanyi. Moti set my parents up on a blind date. Even though my mother was allowed to live at the home for girls for two years, she was desperate to leave and marry. My father, good-looking, intelligent, competent, and alone, seemed to be what she needed. But my mother was ambivalent.

My father told the story this way:

"I got her address and went to the home for girls to meet her. She wasn't home when I arrived, so I walked around the grounds, asking the other girls about her until I finally found her. I thought she was very nice looking. We went out that day, but I hesitated to contact her again. It seemed that she was not interested in pursuing our relationship. When I succeeded in talking to her again, I told her that I was very distraught, feeling that she didn't want to see me again. I told her that I was constantly thinking of her. I even told her that I had trouble focusing at work and had cut my finger on one of the machines. She was touched by this and reluctantly agreed to see me again. After that second date, she wanted to marry me. She was desperate to leave the home for girls. I took her out on a date and showed her my small, one-room apartment in Tel Aviv. Unfit for the two of us, it had a kitchen that I shared with others in the house, and the only bathroom was outside. She didn't care. She thought it was perfect, so we married one month after we first met."

My parents married on July 13, 1949, approximately four years after the war had ended. Four years later, in 1953, my brother Michael was born. He was given the name Moishe after my father's father. When Moishe was two years old, my father decided that the name Moishe was "too Jewish" and would have to be changed. At the age of two, my brother became Michael, or Micha-el, as we called him in Hebrew. My sister, Elizabeth, Elisheva, named after my mother's mother Ester, was born in 1957. My mother glowed with pride after Liz was born, as the neighborhood mothers of mostly baby boys envied her new female arrival.

I was born eighteen months later in 1958 and was called Keti in Hebrew. My mother often told me that I was a surprise, an unwanted pregnancy.

"Life with Daddy was so difficult," she said. "The last thing I needed was to bring another child into this home."

She also went on to say how happy she was that I had been born and how jealous the neighborhood mothers were now that she had two girls. The words didn't bother me because I always felt my mother's love.

I was barely five when we left, so I have few memories of Israel and almost no recollection of friends, family life, or home. Most of my memories have to do with specific things I had seen, heard, and smelled as well as foods I had tasted. I remember large fields of knee-high red poppies that surrounded me in a beautiful park. I remember the beach at Tel Aviv and the excitement of it, including the frozen banana ice cream bars and the chocolate domes filled with soft marshmallow that they sold there. I remember my fourth birthday party, where I sat with friends at the side entrance of the house and ate pretzels. I remember the sweet taste of the homegrown peanuts, which grew on an underground vine in the backyard, and the joy of picking them. I remember the charcoaled potatoes we roasted on sticks on an open campfire and how delicious they were, especially the charred peel. I remember the weekend retreats at Bela's farm in Quiryat Yehuda. Bela was my mother's first cousin, the son of my mother's father's brother who died in World War I. I believe these retreats were meant to be respites from my father because he never came along, or maybe he simply refused to participate. The farm was my fondest memory, perhaps because of the activities or perhaps because there I felt the sense of calm that was the result of being without my father. The farm had chickens, cows, and horses.

In the morning, I went with my older cousin Yitzchok to the chicken coop to carefully pick up the eggs that had rolled down into the semicircular, metal canal below. Sometimes we were allowed to milk the cows. On special occasions, I was allowed to ride on the horse-and-buggy with Bela to bring the fresh milk into town. Lastly, and most vividly, I remember frequent visits to my mother's best friend and relative through marriage, Ester Kostolitz, at her home in Ramat Gan. Ester remained my mother's most loyal friend until the day my mother died.

We left Israel for America in 1963. I was almost five; my sister, Elizabeth, six; and my brother, Michael, barely twelve. We were off on our secret journey to the land of opportunity. Without a word or an explanation, we were uprooted. My father had decided that it was best not to tell us of the plans because if we leaked the information about our move, it could jeopardize the sale of our house or the transfer of finances. With that thought, he decided not to tell us anything.

We left without goodbyes or any opportunity to seal our friendships. We stayed in a hotel in Tel Aviv for a week or two until it was time to go. When my father finally told us what we were doing, we cried hysterically, not wanting to leave. Stunned, we began our eleven-day journey to America on a ship named the *Jerusalem*.

My voyage on the *Jerusalem* was an experience of mostly fear, mixed with acts of kindness from a few caring adults. There were practice rescue operations that were indistinguishable to me from the real thing. Every so often, all the passengers were required to go through emergency practice drills. We donned our life preservers and stood against the perimeter of the ship until the crew fulfilled its drill requirements. I was petrified. I was sure I would be required to jump. There was no convincing me otherwise. I could not be comforted by anyone except a young man in uniform who worked on the ship. As I stood there and cried in fear, he gave me an apple. I understood it as a token of affection and an unspoken "It will be OK." Until then, I had felt as though I had been standing there alone, waiting to walk the plank with no one there to help or comfort me.

It was on this trip that I first experienced performance anxiety. During the final days of the journey, the children on board the ship put on a show. The parents would be entertained as they lounged on the ship's deck. The performance was *Hava Nagila,* and I, the youngest, was chosen to sing solo as my sister danced with a group of girls. I repeatedly told the children's leader that I did not want to sing alone and that I wanted to dance with my sister instead. This children's leader did not take me seriously and made up her mind that I was going to sing. I made up my mind that I was definitely, undoubtedly, positively, absolutely not going to sing. When the time came, we stood on the deck ready to perform as parents lounged and listened to the loudspeakers, and the nice lady announced that we would perform *Hava Nagila.* The dancers were introduced, and then she announced that I would sing. I was terrified. As I stood there and cried, I thought, *You see, lady, I told you I wouldn't sing.*

In 1963, families leaving Israel were only allowed to take one hundred dollars in cash with them. My father had sold our house in Israel at S'deroth Ben Zvi-5,

Ramat Gan for ten thousand dollars. He needed to get that money to America, but it would have been illegal for him to take it out of the country. The Canadian man who purchased the house was instructed to fill a suitcase with one hundred dollar bills and take it to the travel agent, Mrs. Winters, who was helping us emigrate from Israel. She handled the transaction, and the money arrived in America shortly after we did. A few days after arriving in Boro Park, Brooklyn, in June 1963, my father and his first cousin Ritzu went to see a local rabbi; the rabbi instructed them to go to a local bank to pick up a check for the ten thousand dollars.

We were welcomed into the Hungarian Orthodox community of Boro Park by my mother's Orthodox Jewish first cousin Arunka Moskowitz and her family of seven children. The Moskowitzes had five boys, George, Mendi, Moishe, Shuli, and Avi, and two girls, Rose and Hannah. As newcomers, we were generously offered a two-bedroom apartment on the fourth floor of the four-story, walk-up apartment building they owned. My father chose a bedroom for himself, and the remaining four of us were left to negotiate who would win the other bedroom. The outcome: my sister and I shared the bedroom with my mother, and my brother slept on the living room couch. My parents didn't share a bedroom then or any other time during my childhood.

Our new home in Boro Park was exciting. I instantly had a big, live-in family that provided the central gathering place for the rest of the Rothfeld family. I had twelve new second cousins. Aside from the Moskowitz children in the building, I had Paula and Eileen Rothfeld from the Bronx. I also had Debbie, Lea, and Michael Rothfeld from Ontario. I was so excited when they came to visit.

Aside from the four oldest Moskowitz children, we children were all about the same age as the other children in the building as well. Our four-story walk-up was attached to another four-story building. The only difference was that ours was strictly Jewish Orthodox— except for us—and the adjoining building was non-Jewish, mostly Italian. We children played together regardless of our differences. For hours and hours, Orthodox Jews and Italian Catholics played together. I had an Orthodox best friend in my building, Julie Shapiro, and an Italian best friend, Maryann Hamel, in the other building.

We had simple childhood fun. We played traditional inner-city games, which never required anything more than a twenty-five-cent Spalding ball, some chalk, and Popsicle sticks. My favorite game was "Sticks," in which we spaced three tree branches horizontally and evenly on the sidewalk. We had to step between them, and after everyone had a turn, we spread the sticks a little farther apart. If we stepped on a stick, we were out. Eventually, the sticks would be spaced so far apart that we had to jump over them.

The other game we played required a Popsicle stick and a Spalding ball. We placed the Popsicle stick on the line between two concrete squares on the sidewalk. My opponent and I stood at opposite ends of the two squares. We alternately took turns trying to hit the stick with the ball so that the stick moved closer and closer to the opponent's side. Whoever got the stick closest to the opponent won the game.

In the 1960s, Boro Park was a bustling neighborhood and home to many Orthodox and Hassidic Hungarian refugees. My mother frequently took my sister and me to the many shops on Thirteenth Avenue, the main shopping area and the center of town. We mostly shopped for food. On special occasions, we stopped at John's Bargain Store. The treat was a falafel or slice of pizza and some raw peas from the fruit stand.

My favorite shop was a fancy toy store somewhere around Fifty-first Street and Thirteenth Avenue. I knew by its fancy appearance and the quality of the toys in the window that it was off limits to me. My mother steered us away from that store because the prices were more than she could afford. I knew better than to ask, and I accepted that. On rare occasions, we fussed enough and would be allowed to go into the store to browse. The shop had meticulously stacked shelves and beautifully boxed dolls, with real looking doll carriages that were perfectly lined up in the front of the store. I dreamed, but I knew that a doll with a carriage was not possible.

Once, for a birthday, I did get to buy a small doll in a box. She was special, not like the others from John's Bargain Store. She was quality.

My childhood adventures taught me the love of window-shopping and browsing. This habit was imprinted in my neurons. It was all right to look but not to buy. Like so many other lessons of childhood, I learned to make window-shopping a pleasure all its own. My husband jokes about how I spend hours shopping but never buying. I enjoy the looking, hoping, and wishing.

My second favorite store was a children's clothing store. I don't think I ever set foot inside it, but it didn't matter because I wasn't after what was inside. The baby mannequins used to display clothes in the window attracted me. They looked real. I walked down the avenue, always anticipating the moment when we arrived at that store. My mother liked to frequent the bargain store next door, so as she shopped for bargains, I'd venture down the block until I could lay my eyes on those life-sized beauties. I stared and stared until my mother came to retrieve me. I wanted one of those mannequins in the worst way. I can't explain the force that attracted me to that store, but I always looked forward to reaching it. Time and time again, I stopped at that window, contemplating how, if I were lucky enough, I could purchase such a mannequin. I knew that even if we could afford one, they weren't for sale. They were for the window display, but I kept dreaming that one day, somehow, someway I would own one just like that. I yearned to hold that lifelike baby "doll."

In Boro Park, at the age of about seven or eight, I first realized that my father was no ordinary man. As I said before, we lived in my mother's cousin's building. The youngest cousin, Avi, was born a few years after we moved into the building. His baby carriage was kept in the small entrance hall on the ground floor. Someone accidentally threw a cigarette into the stored carriage one day, and it started a small fire in the hall. The firefighters arrived and insisted that everyone go outside. Everyone was evacuated from the building—except my father.

"I'll be there in a minute," he said, but he didn't come out.

The firefighters went in after him as all the people from the building, including my cousins and friends, waited and waited for more then fifteen minutes. He finally emerged from the building holding the large brown suitcase that we had used on our journey from Israel.

I was so embarrassed. He was different from the other fathers standing on the sidewalk. He stood out. Everyone else instinctively knew that this was a small fire that was not going to cause much damage, but for safety, they all got out quickly. My father didn't think in the same way as everyone else. His priorities and sense of logic differed from the norm. In his mind, he was the *hacham*, or wise man, who had all his important possessions with him just in case. To me, he was simply strange.

In Boro Park, it wasn't long before I realized that, as a second cousin, I was not fully accepted by the larger clan of aunts, uncles, and cousins. Although we weren't rejected, we were not accepted with the same enthusiasm that the first cousins had for one another. I don't think it was intentional or malicious, but there were so many of them that they had no real need for us. Or perhaps it was because we were different. But it was hurtful. They were all religious and attended yeshiva, and we did not. We didn't conform to the same social rules. Their gatherings contained plenty of children to play with, so we were simply overlooked or excluded.

Once, when the cousins were visiting, we were all invited to go to their Uncle Mendel's (my mother's first cousin's) house. Already a teenager, my brother declined most family invitations. My father refused to go. So, as was often the case with family outings, my mother, my sister, and I went alone. I felt special there because, before immigrating to the United States, Mendi and his wife, Yaffa, had lived near us in Israel. They spoke Hebrew, and because we were the only children in the family who spoke Hebrew, I felt a special bond. They lived a few blocks from us in Boro Park; we lived on Fifty-fifth Street between Thirteenth and Fourteenth Avenue, and they lived on Fifty-fifth Street between Fourteenth and Fifteenth Avenue.

The day was pure delight. We watched Mendi and Yaffa's movie of their recent trip to Israel. I had not seen or heard anything about Israel since our departure three years earlier, and I was thrilled. The atmosphere was celebratory, and everyone was excited.

Before we left, Mendi gave each visiting cousin one dollar, but he handed my sister and me one dime each. It was confirmed. We were not equal. I wanted so much to be like them, to be a part of the larger Rothfeld family. They were Americanized because they were born in America, and they were happy. They were a family who had a good time together. I desperately craved the simple family happiness that did not exist in our home.

Within a few years, my mother's sisters, Molvin and Reli, arrived in America from Hungary with their children, my first cousins. They were not exactly what I had in mind when I wished for cousins, but I knew that they were mine. They had strange names like Kotika, Yutka, and Osci. They didn't speak English and were all a bit older than I was. I longed for the playmates that I had hoped my second cousins would be, but I accepted what I had and made the best of it. I was about eight years old.

My mother's sister, Reli, who had been with her on the final days of the journey in Magdeburg, was the mother of my two cousins: Yutka, a seventeen-year-old girl, and Osci, a fifteen-year-old boy. Reli arrived in America with terminal breast cancer. Immediately upon their arrival, she began treatment for her metastatic disease at Mount Sinai Hospital in New York. She had been diagnosed with breast cancer in Hungary at the age of forty-three, but her cancer was already advanced at the time of her diagnosis. Reli, her husband, and their two children moved into a brownstone walk-up in Williamsburg, Brooklyn.

My father never visited any of my mother's relatives, and as I said before, my brother —being a teen— seldom did. However, the three of us, (my mother, my sister, and I) often went to visit them. My mother loved Reli and feared that her death was imminent. She wanted to spend as much time as possible with her sister. Reli died at the age of fifty-three, three years after arriving in America. Her husband, Jeno, had lost his first wife, Blanka, and three young children (two boys and a girl) in Auschwitz. He was a kind man, but he had been so deeply traumatized by his experiences that he visibly bore the burden of his past. He never smiled and seldom talked. He spent the rest of his years sitting in a chair, expressionless. I often wondered what he thought about.

My sister's and my encounters with these family members were just short of sign language. No one spoke English, and my sister and I did not speak Hungarian. So we sat for the typical Hungarian feast of cookies, nuts, and fruit at the cocktail table while my mother talked for hours. Our entertainment was watching Yutka and Osci fight. Osci felt that Yutka, a typical teenage girl of the 1960s, spent too much time in the only bathroom styling her bouffant hair. She teased and sprayed and teased and sprayed until her hair was piled high enough to satisfy her. After we consumed enough of the Hungarian friendship food and were no longer amused by the sibling rivalry, we begged our mother to leave, which was never easy to accomplish. Unlike my father, my mother loved her family and loved to be with them. To this day, it amazes me how many hours those Hungarian refugees could spend in the living room, talking and laughing over cookies, nuts, and a bowl of fruit.

Leaving this family was bittersweet, as it always left me with mixed emotions. I was happy to go, but at the same time, I was going home to face my father and his inevitable interrogation. He had no contact with his family, and he was determined to keep us away from my mother's family. He hated my mother's dying sister and her husband. He hated just about everyone, but he especially hated Reli because Reli was strong. When fighting with my mother, he often referred to Reli as "the witch with a broom." Although weak and dying, Reli loved my mother and hated to see her living in a mentally abusive relationship with my father. When Reli still lived in Hungary, my mother had often written letters to her about the difficulties she was having with my father. Reli had now witnessed the disconnection between my father and his family as well as the control he exercised and the agitation he created. During occasional phone conversations, Reli tried to persuade my mother to take us and leave him.

My father often eavesdropped on our phone conversations, so he heard Reli's persuasive remarks. His mission was to eliminate anyone who could give my mother strength and weaken his power over her. Reli was his nemesis. When Reli died, my father continued to eavesdrop whenever he desired and with anyone he pleased. He especially eavesdropped on Reli's teenage daughter, Yutka, who was of equally strong character. Whether they were my mother's phone calls, my brother's, my sister's, or mine, my father felt it was his right to listen in. We knew he was on the phone, but there wasn't much we could do. Most of the time, he sat idle and listened, collecting ammunition in the same way a chipmunk stores acorns for the winter. But there were times when he was not willing to accept my mother's other relationships or her compassionate phone calls from "the relatives." He would pick up the receiver and sabotage the conversation.

Once, when my father was listening in on my mother's phone conversation with her sister, Molvin, he began yelling "Communist whore, communist whore!" over and over as my mother tried to carry on the conversation. They tried to ignore him and kept on talking, but it was very difficult. Other times, he took the mouthpiece from my school clarinet and blew it into the receiver as hard as he could until my mother had no choice but to end her conversations. From then on, left without a choice, my mother made her family phone calls from the pay phone at the candy store around the corner.

BAY RIDGE, BROOKLYN

My father was never comfortable with my mother's family and his Jewish, Orthodox surroundings. Four years after moving to Boro Park, my parents bought a two-family house in Bay Ridge, a totally Christian neighborhood. I was eight years old, and it was the summer before third grade, a few weeks before the start of school. A few days after we moved in, my father, as the only parent proficient in the English language, took my sister and me to be registered at our new school, P.S. 170. It was the last time my father ever entered any of my schools until my high school graduation. From that point on, my mother handled school communications, using us children as interpreters. My brother continued to go to Shallow Junior High School, the same local junior high he had attended while we lived in Boro Park.

The move to Bay Ridge was exciting. Coming from an apartment, the new house was big. The former owners had left some things behind, and discovering these odd items was like a treasure hunt. There were so many rooms with something left behind in almost every corner. The house had two apartments, a front garden, and a backyard with gorgeous red roses. The neighborhood was full of kids to play with, especially little girls. We took the downstairs apartment and rented the upstairs apartment to a young military couple, Paul and Carol Rosedale. We kids were friendly with the Rosedales and often knocked on their door so that we could play in their apartment. They had a friendly cat named Nobbynose. Paul had just finished military duty in Las Vegas, and they had a genuine nickel slot machine, which they let us play—and even keep our winnings.

It was 1967, and I was eight years old. My favorite show at the time was *Little Miss America*, a beauty pageant held weekly at Palisades Amusement Park. Every week, some fifty girls between the ages of five and ten stood on a stage in angelic white dresses to be judged for beauty. One by one, they walked across the stage and said a few words as the judges looked them over. I envisioned myself as one of those girls and was absolutely convinced that I would be the prettiest and win. One day, I spoke to Carol about wanting to be a contestant in *Little Miss America*. She told me that she had connections and would look into it for me. Nothing ever came of it, but it was fun to imagine.

The unspoken conditions and rules of our new house were made immediately clear by my father. One by one, I learned and conformed to them the best I could. I lived in constant fear that somehow, unknowingly, I would violate these rules and have to suffer the consequences. The rest of the family wasn't as diligent as I was, so I knew that inevitably they would screw up. I believed that it was my obligation and within my power to enforce the rules and see that my father was never agitated. I don't know how my self-appointed position evolved, but taking into account the personalities of the others and their nonexistent relationships with my father, I saw no other way but to take charge.

The rules were as follows:

Rule 1: My brother's "Jewish" friends from the old neighborhood were not welcome into our new home.

In my father's eyes, they were derelicts, imposing their negative attributes on to my brother. Of course, I never saw anything wrong with them. In fact, they all appeared rather nice.

Rule 2: My mother's relatives from Boro Park and Williamsburg, the only family she had and her entire social network, were forbidden. Under no circumstances were they to enter our house.

As a matter of fact, I can count on one hand the number of times my mother's family visited us during my entire childhood. On those rare occasions when they did visit, it was on the sly when my father was not at home. Those few visits were never comfortable because everyone feared that he would return unexpectedly.

Rule 3: If you visited the relatives in Boro Park or Williamsburg, it was best not to tell him. He hated them.

As I mentioned before, he blamed my mother's relatives for everything. He believed, in his paranoia, that they had coerced my mother into hating him and had turned my brother against him. None of this was based in reality. His actions did not register in his mind as illogical. He saw no wrong in himself. He was not to blame; it was everyone else's fault. My mother frequently visited her family in Boro Park, and each visit created panic in me. I was terrified as I walked through the door of my house after a visit with the relatives. Even so, I enjoyed Boro Park immensely, and I even liked going to Williamsburg. I felt connected there—to the people, the food, and the family.

Shortly before reaching home, however, I would begin to feel sick to my stomach. I knew my father would be waiting for me, and the interrogation would begin. I always hoped that I would be lucky and that, just once, he wouldn't be home… or wouldn't ask… or wouldn't notice me. But he was usually lying in wait for me.

He would start with "Where did you go?" whenever I walked in, as if he didn't know. If I was too vague, he steered me to admit that I had been to "the relatives in Boro Park." He wouldn't use their names. I would know by his look that he wasn't pleased, and often he would fight with my mother. We had broken Rule 3, and now we had to pay by enduring either his extreme agitation or the silent treatment.

One encounter particularly sticks out in my mind. I couldn't have been more than nine years old, but I can still feel the fear and panic. My cousin Kathy (Kotika) had just arrived from Hungary a few weeks earlier. She was about thirteen. I wasn't pleased, but my mother had arranged for her to spend the day with me at our house.

I knew from the start that this was not a good idea; I was about to violate Rule 2: "The cousins from Boro Park are not welcome in our house." Every now and then, my mother mustered up the courage to defy my father. This time, however, she left me holding the bag.

The newly immigrated cousin spoke almost no English. I chanted in my head over and over again: *Please go home before he comes home from work.* I watched every passing minute on the clock. My body was there, but my mind was frozen. I couldn't focus on anything except that she was still there and that the time of my father's arrival was rapidly approaching. Then it was too late.

I heard the key in the door. My heart pounded. I was panic-stricken. I waved her under the dining room table and told her in gestures that she had to hide under it. She followed my lead. As my father walked in, he noticed Kathy right away. To my shock and good fortune, he was extremely nice and welcoming to her; on rare occasions, he could be quite charming. Kathy came out, and they had a nice little conversation in Hungarian. It was a rare moment, but I was already traumatized from the anticipation and sense of impending doom. I was also sure that Kathy was equally traumatized by the experience.

Rule 4: No one, under any circumstance, was to enter my father's room, eat his food, or touch his possessions without permission.

In our home, my father lived in solitary confinement as though he were fighting a solitary war. His room was his barracks, and we were the enemies. He hoarded his food and wrote *Abba*, which means father, on everything in the refrigerator. We knew what the *Abba* label meant, but he wasn't shy about also inscribing the words *Do not touch*. Occasionally, I found the courage and felt hungry enough to ask if I could have one of his TV dinners. He wouldn't be pleased, but he would agree to give it up.

His acquiescence usually meant that I would be sent on a mission to buy him replacements. These missions were never easy because my father possessed two qualities that, in sum, made him heartless: he was cheap, and he lacked empathy.

My father worked only two blocks from the A&P supermarket, but that didn't matter because replacing his food was my punishment for eating the TV dinner as well as a bizarre demonstration of loyalty to him. He wasn't going to the supermarket. It was my mission. After school, I had to go to the A&P and do his food shopping so that he could restock his "Do not touch" supplies. Often, he would add a twist. There were two A&P supermarkets, and I was directed not to go to the closer one because he was convinced that the Campbell's chicken and rice soup was a penny cheaper at the more distant store. Off I would go to the A&P of his fancy. This pattern continued throughout my days in public school and on into college. As a young adult, I would return home from CCNY in Harlem after an hour-and-fifteen-minute train ride, obediently taking the local train instead of my usual express so that I could get off at the proper A&P and return home with the cans of soup. Panic set in when the supermarket was missing something he had sent me to buy. When this happened, my father treated me as though I had personally failed. He was angry, disappointed, and did not believe me. He was convinced that this was my personal failure.

I quickly realized that I had better get it right the first time, or else I would pay for my mistake by going on a make-up mission the following day. I learned not to return home until I had searched the entire neighborhood looking for exactly what he wanted, even if it meant going all over town, spending my own money, and pretending I had bought the food from "his store."

Rule 5: The neighbors were not to sit on his steps or enter his backyard.

I panicked if one of the girls next door stepped on our stoop to say hello or if a neighbor's kid's ball went into our backyard. I quickly intervened before my father saw them. That way he wouldn't have to stick his head out the window and scream. I knew that he spent long periods peeping through the Venetian blinds, waiting to attack. He was like a mad dog, looking for someone or something to lunge at.

Our two-family house was attached to another two-family house. We each had our own six-step stoop, and there was a common one-foot slab that we shared at the top of the steps. The Italian girls next door, Rosemarie, Lena, Joanne, and Phyllis were my age, and I liked them. My father became agitated when they sat on his six inches of the one-foot slab or when their friends occasionally spilled over to our stoop. He installed a fence around the stoop and across the top of the one-foot slab so that each family was left with six inches to sit on. After that, we spoke to one another as we sat on our six-inch slab and peered through the fence like inmates. It was embarrassing, but by that time, everyone knew my father and no one was surprised. The neighbors, always nice and accepting, adored my mother. Her friendly, caring personality made up a bit for his shortcomings. Because the neighbors felt sorry for my mother and us children, they went out of their way to be kind to us.

Our home was a two-bedroom, railroad apartment. Just as before, my father dictated which bedroom was his; once again, the rest of us would have to bargain for the remaining bedroom. My sister and I won the bedroom, but we would have to share it with my mother. As in Boro Park, my mother had no personal space. Now that we were a little older, my sister and I were embarrassed to share a bedroom with our mother, but we never questioned it because there was no choice. Our mother had never—and would never—share a room with our father. It had been this way as long as we could remember. I adored my mother and felt comforted by her, so this arrangement wasn't hard to accept. We hoped the neighborhood kids wouldn't notice, but my father often left the door open to his room, and it was quite obvious that there was only one twin-sized bed in there for him.

My father's bedroom was an embarrassment. From the day we moved in, it had blue, flowered wallpaper that was never changed. His bed was actually an army-style cot. The mattress sagged, so for added support, he put a few pieces of wall paneling underneath it, which were clearly visible at the edges. The bed was pushed up against the outside wall, which made him feel cold. He was always worried about "catching a draft," so this arrangement was not good. To prevent the draft, he nailed a cord to the wall and placed scraps of wall paneling between the bed and the wall. Under the bed sat two basins. One was an old, white, enameled basin for his personal washing; the other was made of green plastic and used for mopping. His daily routine was to fill his personal washbasin with water from the bathroom and return to his room, place the basin on a folding chair, and take care of his personal hygiene in his room. He washed military style in a basin instead of using a shower or tub the way most people do. Once in a while, he took a bath, but I don't recall him ever taking a shower.

Although he usually washed in his bedroom, he sometimes took the washbasin into the bathroom and washed there, placing the washbasin over the toilet. We had only one bathroom in the house and when he used it, he would stay in it for a long, long time. No matter how badly we had to use the bathroom, he did not come out. We would bang, scream, kick, beg, and cry, but there was little chance that he was going to open the door and come out. In the early years, we used a potty that my experienced mother brought with us from Israel, but that was not a possibility as we got older.

The bathroom was across from our bedroom. I awoke on many mornings to my mother's pleading cries as she banged repeatedly on the bathroom door while my father ignored her from behind the closed door.

In her anguished Hungarian, I'd hear her beg, "Ain occurum menunk a vetsi," meaning "I need to go to the bathroom."

After an excruciating length of time, he would emerge looking disgusted and aggravated, finally allowing my mother to use the bathroom.

When I was in that house, I was angry with my mother for not having better control. Why couldn't she play by the rules like I did? Didn't she know that he was not to be disturbed? Didn't she know that he should be left to do whatever he wanted and however he wanted to do it regardless of the consequences?

The walls of my father's bedroom were decorated with cards that we (mostly I) had sent to him over the years to "prove our love." They were largely school-made valentines or Father's Day cards. One day, I found a Valentine's Day card that my sister, Liz, had made for him at school when she was ten and in the fourth grade. For years, he proudly displayed that card, but this was no typical Valentine's Day card from a daughter to a father. It read as follows:

> Dear Daddy,
> Happy Valentine's Day. I love you.
> Do you like me? When are you going to buy us Baby Magic?
>
> Yours truly,
> Elizabeth

It was innocent and honest because she really wasn't sure if our father liked her. It was a clear statement of how we felt. My father laminated the card and kept it as verification that he had bought us Baby Magic, the hottest doll of the 1970s. He was incapable of acknowledging the significant pain in my sister's words.

My father's feelings for my sister were made clear in a photograph that he framed and hung on his bedroom wall. It was a picture taken on Easter Sunday of me, my sister, and two neighborhood friends, Mary and Victoria, wearing our new "Easter outfits." But before he framed it, my father placed a homemade mat on the picture with a hole that only allowed me to be seen; he covered my sister and the two other girls. He surrounded me with colorful star stickers, the kind that a teacher puts on tests for a good performance. He continues to proudly display this picture in his apartment, and I find it extremely disturbing.

The truth is, I don't think he likes her less or me more. I don't think he is capable of liking at all. But my sister, unlike me, did not care about the rules, and he couldn't handle her rebellion or nonconformity. He often accused her of "trying to influence me," which of course meant that she might give me strength to rebel, as my mother's family and my brother's friends had given them.

On the same wall were American Legion certificates. Later, he added articles and awards from my career as a nurse at Mount Sinai. My sister referred to it as "Kathy's shrine," and she was right. This wall didn't celebrate my accomplishments, though. It celebrated *his* triumphs because he felt that anything good was a result of what he had done, not what I had achieved or deserved.

On the desk in his room, he meticulously lined up pens, tape, notes, forks, spoons, aftershave, scissors, crackers, glasses, and whatever else he could fit on it. Although horribly cluttered, the surface was meticulously ordered with items arranged like little soldiers. He had a system for everything. He tied his wallet with numerous rubber bands. If a rubber band snapped as he was putting it back on, he would become very upset and curse under his breath. I knew the "systems" and tried very hard not to mess them up. Unfortunately, a lot of his systems were more like booby traps, with strings and wires holding everything together.

Trying to follow his systems was like being the mouse in a game of "Mouse Trap." He set oven grills with attached bells into the living room and dining room windows as "mock" window guards to keep intruders out. The Venetian blinds were so old they barely worked. As I struggled to open one, I ran the risk of breaking the cord or, worse yet, having it fall from the window altogether. The wobbly TV stand, which should have been trashed years earlier, barely supported the weight of the TV because my father had done a shoddy repair job, using L-brackets and screws to hold it together. He watched every move we made, waiting for us to mess something up. I carefully walked around the house, trying not to touch anything so that the inevitable wouldn't happen.

But it often did happen: the dreaded "system failure." Something would break or fall apart and trigger his anger and criticism.

And then he'd let us have it. We earned an instant "Laci look." That was what we kids used to call the angry, agitated look he made whenever something went wrong. He pursed his lips, his eyes grew cold, and he

walked past us sometimes for days—and even weeks—
at a time, avoiding eye contact. Very often, he mumbled
a string of Hungarian curse words under his breath as he
walked near. I know them all too well: *Oz onyat petchio*,
Budosh corvonet, and *Menu a fronzbo*. Translations: "your
mother's vagina," "whore," and "Go to hell."

No matter how tenuous or fragile the elements of
his system were, he never saw the reality of the situation.
His was a "perfect" system, and somehow we failures
had messed with it. It was always our fault. If it was
something I did, touched, or mistreated, he'd say, "Next
time, let me do it," looking as agitated as though I had
broken a window.

<hr />

Throughout my childhood, my father rarely hired
anyone to do work around our house. He believed he
could do it all, but he couldn't do any of it very well. Once
or twice, he allowed my mother to hire a professional to
paint and put up wallpaper. If he couldn't fix something,
it would simply stay broken.

He repaired his own shoes. Sometimes that meant
putting a piece of cardboard inside as an insole, but
most of the time he repaired the sole. He bought his
own leather and nails and went to work. He even had
a tool that looked like a giant jack from the game of
jacks to put the shoe on as he repaired it. His frugality
included not buying new shoes. Instead, he placed metal

taps on the heels, and we heard the metal nails scraping along the sidewalk as he walked. The metal taps gave his shuffle a unique sound so that we clearly knew when he was coming. In later years, he put taps on his sneakers, too. That sound was particularly irritating, like chalk squeaking on a blackboard. But the sneakers lasted, and that was all that mattered.

He protected his clothing in the same way. He was fond of—or rather, obsessed with—a few articles of clothing, mostly dark blue, and those were the only garments he wore. He rarely washed them because he feared that laundering them would cause them to wear out more quickly. We had to tolerate the smell. When he did wash his clothes, it had to be by hand, which he did himself. The washing machine was out of the question. Machine washing would certainly cause them to deteriorate before their projected twenty years.

Occasionally, I would buy him something new for his birthday, hoping that he would appear in something "normal." But it didn't matter. Not only did he not wear the new pieces of clothing, he used them as weapons against me.

As he expected, I would obediently buy him gifts for his birthday and Christmas. He would admire the gift, then put it neatly back into the box, and place it in a hall closet that belonged solely to him. Like his room, the closet was off limits to the rest of the family.

The next time I failed on one of his missions or broke one of the "rules"—perhaps not buying him exactly what he needed, yawning as he spoke, visiting my mother's relatives, or not keeping my brother in check—I would find the still-boxed gift that I had bought days, weeks, or months earlier thrown on top of the dining room table. This was his message to me that I had failed. His rejection made me feel guilty, so I would try harder to please him. I did whatever it took: listened to his stories of Sophocles or Spinoza while I desperately wanted to be outside with my friends, fixed the roof or toilet with him for hours, or pretended to like him. When he was satisfied and felt that he had received enough attention, he took back the gift, only to neatly store it again—still boxed— in that little closet, all ready for its next mission.

Somehow, even after repeated insults, I couldn't comprehend his strategy. I always went back for more, never learning from previous experience. He expected something from me, and I needed to comply. That was our pattern.

I was always hopeful for a different outcome; maybe this time he would act with acceptance, kindness, and gratitude. But each time it was the same. I knew the repertoire by heart. It was predictable. I would pretend that maybe my gift would make him "happy" and he would not reject it—and thus, me. He anticipated a gift, as it was my obligation. By complying, I was providing him with ammunition, and I knew it. He had something significant that he could control and use to hurt me. He wasted no time and did so at the first opportunity.

Giving him a gift was a horror because I knew that it gave him the means to start the cycle again. No matter how many times it happened, and there were many, I never got used to the rejection. For much of my life, gift giving was a difficult task. It could take me hours or days and repeated trips to stores to decide on a gift for someone, especially for him. I debated and thought and debated: *It was of no use. Too cheap. Not the right style. Inappropriate. Too much for the house. Too much about the self. They have too many.* After hours and hours, I finally chose. I comforted myself with *OK, it can be returned,* and I fully expected that it would be.

I also had to think very carefully about the card that went along with my father's gift. My father always carefully examined the picture on the card, and he became agitated if it was a picture of an animal, especially a dog or a horse. He would look at the dog or horse and say, "So what do you think? I am a dog?" or "You know what a jackass is? A horse." Instead, he wanted flowers, something nice, something pretty. Masculine cards don't usually come with flowers, and even if they did, I didn't associate flowers with him.

Choosing cards for his birthday or Father's Day became harder as I got older. Naturally, most of the cards had nice things to say, such as "You taught me so much" or "You are the best father any girl could wish for." Not being able to buy a card with a dog or a horse and then finding one that was also appropriate to the way I felt about him made the task nearly impossible. I learned to hone in on the same type of card for every occasion: the one they make for kids who don't really like their parents. It has a country scene with an emotionless, generic saying like "Happy Birthday. Wishing all your dreams come true."

Like a railroad train, you could walk from the front of our downstairs apartment to the back in one straight line, through the rooms rather than down a hallway. My brother had an eight-by-ten-foot room, which was more like a vestibule, in the front of the apartment. To get to the bedrooms, we first had to walk through his room and then through the living room, the dining room, and past the kitchen. After a few years, my brother demanded his privacy and was given the second bedroom. My sister, my mother, and I were evicted to the dining room.

We were Jews in a Christian neighborhood, speaking two strange languages, Hebrew and Hungarian. Our parents never slept together and always fought. Now, to add to all that oddness, my sister and I slept in the dining room with our mother.

It was about to get worse. One of our favorite home-alone "dining room" activities was jumping from the top of the dresser on to the bed. Eventually, we broke the bed. For the next year, we slept on a mattress on the dining room floor.

Because it was a railroad apartment, anyone who entered had to pass the dining room. Fortunately, when friends came over, we spent most of the time in the finished basement, which had its own entrance at the back of the house, so we could bypass the dining room altogether. Trouble came when friends had to use the bathroom; there was no choice but to let them go upstairs.

I desperately wanted to have a "normal family." Why couldn't we be like the families on *Leave It to Beaver* or *Father Knows Best*? I was distressed and exhausted. It took so much energy to control it all, to try to "look normal." Our lives in Bay Ridge were far from normal, but my sister and I tried hard to fit in. Fortunately, in that lower-middle-class neighborhood, the neighbors were mostly nice, accepting families. Without a doubt, we were unusual, but we were welcomed.

Since my brother remained at Shallow Junior High School in the old school district he continued to have contact with friends from the "old neighborhood," which of course infuriated my father and broke Rule 1.

My sister and I, by then aged nine and eleven and social, soon found the neighborhood girls and established friendships. There were many girls living on our one-square city block: Renee Caravello, Marybeth and Jeanne Pugliese, Mary Dunat, Gail and Irene Katen, Victoria Greco, and Lillian Cherico.

Lillian was a year younger than I, and I was extremely envious of her. She had four brothers, a cabana at

Breezy Point, and coordinating Danskin outfits in every imaginable color for every day of the week. Those outfits with solid shorts and striped tops were the hottest girls' clothes in the late 1960s, and they were not cheap. I yearned for just one outfit, but my mother didn't see how they were worth the cost, and she wasn't willing to spend the money. So, for my ninth or tenth birthday, I put together all my birthday money and bought myself my first pair of brown Danskin shorts and an imitation brown, striped shirt to go with it. I was delighted.

It wasn't just expensive, trendy clothes that my mother refused to buy. Sometimes she refused to buy simple necessities like shoes. In the sixties, we were not allowed to wear sneakers to school, so we wore Mary Janes, the fancy patent leather shoes that sometimes came in velvet. One problem with Mary Janes was that the soles were very thin, so the soles were completely worn within a few months. Because they were our only school shoes, we couldn't even send them to the shoemaker. They were soon beyond repair. My mother engaged in an ongoing battle with my father as to who was going to pay for new shoes because my father only gave her fifteen dollars a week.

My mother either didn't have the extra money to pay for shoes, or she simply refused to spend it. We were too frightened to ask my father, so we became resourceful. We wore the shoes until a hole broke right through the sole. Like our father had done with his shoe repair, we inserted a piece of cardboard into the shoe, which usually worked until it rained or snowed. We changed the cardboard after we wore through that too or until it got saturated by the rain or snow. Sooner or later, my mother gave in and bought us new shoes, but it was never easy.

In the new neighborhood, we were quickly taught the "girl's hierarchy." A woman named Eileen was at the top of the pecking order. Eileen was the official babysitter for sisters Gail and Irene Katen, and as we soon learned, Eileen was the neighborhood gatekeeper for little girls. She lived around the corner, a few doors down from the Katens. She was about twenty-one and an only child living with her elderly parents in a two-family house. Her two unmarried, elderly aunts lived in the apartment upstairs.

The Katen girls also had the privilege of frequenting Eileen's home and hanging out with her on the stoop. She bought everyone birthday and Christmas gifts and occasionally took the Katens as well as the other neighborhood girls for outings to places like Coney Island, Palisades Amusement Park, and Chinatown. There was a lot of excitement to be had if you were "in" with Eileen. To be included, my sister and I would have to figure out a way in. My first thought was to have Eileen as a babysitter, but our parents never went out. They never even really spoke to each other, so thinking that they might go out was hopeless.

We had to be a little assertive yet nonchalantly work our way into the girls' group. But Eileen was no normal twenty-one-year-old. She didn't hang out with other twenty-one-year-olds. She didn't even hang out with eighteen-year-olds.

The neighborhood girls who we had hoped would be our friends were her friends, her social circle, all of them between the ages of eight and twelve. Little by little, we worked our way in so that we could hang out with the rest of the girls and Eileen on the local meeting ground: Eileen's stoop. Night after night, day after day, we headed for Eileen's stoop.

Eileen, I realized even at that young age, was needy like my father. There was clearly something wrong with her. She had demanding and bizarre behaviors. Why the parents—hers and all of ours—didn't recognize that or question her motives for befriending ten-year-old girls was curious. She also had a deceptive side that made parents overlook her other character flaws. Anyone who knew Eileen knew that she was a high-maintenance person and needed to be in control. Her self-esteem needed to be constantly stroked. I walked on eggshells around her just to "stay in the club." But sooner or later, she struck out at me, and my respite from home became another nightmare.

The girls came around the corner to my house to deliver the message: "Eileen says you can't come to her house because you contradicted her." My response at nine was that I didn't even know what *contradicted* meant. They talked me into going over to request clarification, which I did. As I approached, Eileen angrily pointed her finger at me as she told me that I had contradicted her and that I was not welcome to come hang around her house anymore. As I tried to understand what I was being accused of, she pointed out to everyone else that they should note how I was doing it again. I was dismissed and not to come back. I was doomed: no friends to play with.

At first I kept away, but that became unbearable. Without entry to Eileen's kingdom, I was nothing. There was no place else to go. All the girls were there. I walked around the block over and over, hoping that she or my friends would take pity on me, recognize my loneliness, and draw me back in. No such luck.

Across the street from Eileen's house, the teenagers sat on Mary Dunat's stoop. They felt sorry for me and understood the absurdity of Eileen's behavior, so they let me sit with them. In the 1960s, sitting with the "hippie" teenagers was a real privilege. Many of them were the older brothers and sisters of my friends. My friends were absolutely forbidden by their older siblings to linger on the stoop any longer than it took to walk out the front door and down the steps. From across the street where I sat, I watched with envy as my friends sat on Eileen's stoop.

After days that seemed like weeks, Eileen was ready to negotiate. Across the street came an informant: "Eileen says that she will let you come back if you apologize." *Apologize for what?* I thought. I never even knew what Eileen's accusation was. An apology would not be enough, though. Eileen wanted more. The informant revealed that I would have to cry to convince Eileen of my sincerity. Those were the conditions, and she would accept nothing less.

That was difficult, as I was not a crier. I had mastered the art of being emotionally stoic. Crying did not come easily to me, but with some work and my desperation to go back to the stoop, I managed to cry or at least do a good job of faking it. The turmoil was finally over. But I knew it would not last because Eileen targeted my sister and me in hostile attacks, probably because we had no one to advocate for us. If she had treated the other girls in that way, she certainly would have had to deal with their hot-tempered mothers on her stoop.

Time went by, and by the age of twelve or thirteen, when my sister and I became more independent, we shed Eileen from our lives. She continued to send holiday cards to my father, who repeatedly told me what a nice person she was and how she continued to ask about my sister and me. "Why don't you send her a card?" my father would say. My standard response was "Why don't you tell her to drop dead?"

THE HIDDEN MEZUZAH

My earliest recollection of the Holocaust was at about age six or seven. It seems natural for kids at this age to begin to ask questions about grandparents. I couldn't understand why all my friends had grandparents, and I didn't. It was always the same answer: "They died in Germany." I didn't really understand, but somehow I knew by my mother's reaction that something terrible had happened and that I shouldn't ask anymore. It would bring tears to her eyes and a look of pain to her face.

Then there was A-12636, the identity that had been given to my mother in Auschwitz. Living in a non-Jewish neighborhood, it didn't take long to realize that this was not the norm. I would often ask my mother why she had the number tattooed on her arm. Even though I'm sure I knew the answer after asking the first time, I needed constant confirmation that the answer was really the answer. She would say, "It was put there by the Germans," and not much more. Again, from the look on her face, I rarely pursued the issue. My main concern was whether or not it had hurt her. My mother would assure me that having it placed really wasn't that bad. She would tell me that in the early part of the war, the numbers were placed by hand. By the time she had been taken to Auschwitz, they had already started to tattoo numbers by machine for greater speed and efficiency.

At one time during my childhood, I recall my father looking into ways of having the number removed from my mother's arm. After all, we did live in a Christian neighborhood. My father believed that the failure of the Jews of Europe to assimilate was a terrible mistake that had contributed to the Holocaust. Therefore, he personally would not make the same mistake. He tried in every possible way not to be identified as a Jew.

In fact, my father encouraged the opposite. He was delighted to send us to Vacation Bible School at the local Lutheran church as our summer camp program. We colored in Jesus coloring books and learned songs like "Let Us Break Bread Together on Our Knees." He even gladly donated money for the cause. On Sundays, we went to Mass at St. Ephrem's Catholic Church with our friends. I went so often that I learned to recite the "Our Father" by heart, which I can still do proficiently.

I did not know any of the Jewish prayers, but I had mastered the Christian ones. We dressed for Christmas and Easter, not Chanukah and Passover. We never set foot in a synagogue. As a matter of fact, the first time I remember going into a synagogue was around the age of eighteen when I had my first Jewish boyfriend and my first encounter with any secular Jew.

One day, when my father was not home, my mother asked me to come into the entrance hall with her. She took the little step stool from the kitchen and walked toward the entrance hall as I followed behind her, wondering what she was up to. She placed the step stool on the floor and then stood on top of it as she reached above the doorpost to feel for something along the ledge and to the right. I watched as she pulled down a one-and-a-half-inch silver mezuzah secretly concealed above the doorframe.

She said, "I want you to know that this is here. If Daddy knew, he would kill me."

I felt honored to have it on our doorpost. It meant that we belonged to something: the traditions of our ancestors, the Jewish people, and the relatives in Boro Park. From that day on, I have always had a mezuzah on the door of my home.

Eventually, my mother decided against having the tattooed number removed, and I was happy with her decision. To me, it was a symbol of her heroism, her courage, and her suffering. I wanted it to be a message to others to treat her with extra special loving care; she had been taken to the limit and survived. Most of all, I wanted it to be a symbol to the world of the tragedy that had existed, a tragedy the world must never forget. Too many people were denying that the Jewish Holocaust had ever occurred. With the number on her arm, she was living proof of Nazi barbarism to six million Jews.

In our new Bay Ridge home, my father spent most of his time locked in his room. We were content only when he was not at home. The sound of his key in the front door immediately altered the household mood. Leading into our home, there were two outside doors: the outermost locked door and then two inner doors, side by side, one to our apartment and the other to the apartment upstairs. I always panicked when I heard the outer door open. I sat, hopeful that it would be the upstairs tenant, but as the key entered the lock of our apartment door, I had a sick feeling in my stomach because now he was home. We now had to deal with his anger and rejection. It was not unusual for my father to enter the house after work, walk past everyone, and not utter a single word. In fact, it was pretty much the norm. Sometimes, especially when my mother was sleeping on the dining room couch, my father would walk the long way around the dining room table to avoid passing near her.

We dreaded him. He was always irritated and on edge. It wouldn't take much to set him off. All it would take was a few words from my mother or my brother having a friend over. He would become irate, screaming and cursing relentlessly for hours.

He had a routine, and he rarely veered from it because he was a man of rituals. He would come home, make dinner for himself, eat by himself, and then retreat to his room for a few hours of TV in solitary confinement. As soon as his bedroom door closed, I would breathe a sigh of relief.

Ironically, his favorite shows were comedies. He especially liked Laurel and Hardy and the Three Stooges. I couldn't understand it. He never laughed or smiled around us, yet he often allowed himself to have long belly laughs while he watched his shows in his room behind closed doors. As I walked past his bedroom door, it would tear my heart to hear him laugh uncontrollably.

But one day was very different. It was sometime around 1970. One evening, as I walked past my father's room, I heard him crying. I hesitated for a minute, not really wanting to go inside, and then tried the handle to see if the door was unlocked. (He often locked the door even when he was in his room.)

He was sitting on his cot with a bottle of rum near him. This was an unusual sight because my father rarely drank. He was crying as he began to tell me that his younger brother survived the war and was now living in Canada in a mental institution. I felt sorry for him, for his losses, for his wishful thinking, and for the delusion he was experiencing from too much alcohol. I never thought about it again, and he never mentioned it again.

The worst days at home were Sundays. My father often worked overtime on Saturday, so Sunday was his longest day at home. We had to walk around quietly so that we wouldn't set him off into a fit of rage. It took hours for him to prepare his breakfast as he methodically chopped prepared pork sausage and vegetables for his solitary feast while listening to the Christian radio programs that often in themselves were too much to handle. We held our breath until he retreated back to his quarters. Then we could relax again, praying that he would take a nap or watch some television.

On Sundays, I found it more difficult to go out and play. I sensed that I needed to put in extra hours of patrol to mind the fort. In my naive mind, I somehow felt that I had the power to keep it all in check. I couldn't take the chance of leaving my father, mother, and brother all together—unsupervised—for too long. It was simply too risky. Fighting between my mother and father or my brother and father could break out at any time, and it could be ugly. The neighbors would hear the yelling, my mother would scream and cry, and my father would damn my mother and her relatives before retreating into an angry silence. During the worst fights, my father and brother would get physical. I knew I would have to stick around or at least check in frequently.

Then one day, I let my guard down. It was the summer after sixth grade, and my best friend, Renee Caravello, was moving to Hicksville, New York. I had never known anyone who lived outside of the city. Although I was sad to lose my friend, I was excited about having someone to visit in the country—as I considered Long Island. Shortly after she moved, my sister and I were invited to spend the weekend at her new home. We were so excited!

We both knew it would be risky to leave my mother, father, and brother unattended. After some hesitation, we decided to go and check in daily by telephone. On Saturday, when we telephoned home, I heard screaming and fighting in the background. My father was yelling something about my brother beating him with a stick, and the police were at our house.

Full of fear, my sister and I knew we had to go home. My brother had again become agitated by my father and had threatened him with a wooden bed slat. My father called the police and claimed, "He tried to kill me."

My sister and I had to continually determine whether it would be worth it to leave them unattended again, and we almost never thought it was. On the rare occasion that one of us had a sleepover, the other stayed at home.

By this time, my father was becoming more and more irritated by my brother's presence in the bedroom next door. He wanted to move my brother to another part of the house—as far away as possible. He could not tolerate my brother's stereo or any other sound he made. Having the two of them living adjacent to each other was risky. My brother had a knack for disturbing my father, and my father was always agitated by something. My brother did not fear him; in fact, he had a look that said, "Go ahead and push me. I dare you. You're the one who'll be sorry." As I learned the weekend I went to my best friend's new home, my brother could lose control.

I was extremely fearful of another confrontation

between my father and brother. As with everything else, I felt it was my duty to prevent it.

My brother moved down to the finished basement, my sister and I got the bedroom, and my mother got a second-hand convertible couch in the dining room. It was a major improvement, and we could now have friends over without humiliation. The house at least *looked* normal.

Soon after my brother turned eighteen, he had a little gift for my father. He took away the only connection they had: my father's last name. My brother legally changed his last name, completing the identity transformation my father had initiated when my brother was two years old. From that day on, they rarely spoke.

TRAPPED

Throughout my childhood, my father often intercepted me on my way out of his bedroom.

As I tried to leave, relieved that I was now liberated from his hold, he would stop me abruptly and say, "Promise me something."

"OK," I'd say. "What?"

"Promise me that if you ever have a boy child, you will not circumcise him."

Stunned and frightened by the words, I stood there wanting to close my ears, but I knew I had no choice. I had to let him go on speaking those horrid words until he was done.

He would continue, "During the war, the Jewish boys would be asked to lower their pants. If they were circumcised, they were immediately identified as Jews and sent to the concentration camps."

I couldn't have been more than ten or eleven years old when he first started this. I could see the terrible scene in my mind's eye, and it scared me. I could picture innocent Jewish boys in some alley being confronted by the SS, the humiliation of having to lower their pants, and the tragic results of the discovery.

My father repeated this same scenario over and over again, and each time was as disturbing as the first. I felt trapped and wished he would stop. I was forced to face the vision that he had created inside my head. It was unbearable.

"Promise me," he would repeat, looking at me for a response before I was allowed to exit.

I had no choice but to say, "I promise."

With those false words came guilt. I knew that with my strong Jewish identity, it was a promise I would most likely not keep. But it was my ticket away from him, and I desperately wanted to end these moments and get back to my friends.

When I had three sons, those words came back to haunt me. I was afraid to tell my father that I was indeed going to have them circumcised. I was also afraid of the embarrassment I would feel when he didn't show up, and if he did show up, I didn't know how he would react. To placate him, I gave my first son, Adam, the middle name Stephan, after my father's brother. I wondered what this ritual would mean for my boys later in life. The seeds had been planted in me, and they were hard to ignore. Whether my father would come to the bris or not, the religious event would be infused with fear and horrible imagery for me.

Because my sister and brother rarely communicated with my father and because he avoided my mother, I was his main contact. I was his child, his partner, his confidante, and—most of all—his caretaker. Through my numerous encounters with him, I learned to be tolerant and stand at attention for what seemed like hours at a time. At first, my mother sent me on what I perceived as "missions of happiness" to see if I could improve my father's spirits.

In Hebrew, my mother would say, "Go and say a few words to him."

It was like going to the dentist or taking a dreaded test. The anticipated event produced tremendous anxiety for me, but knowing that backing out was not an option, I took a deep breath, braced myself, and did my duty to get it over with as soon as possible. I resented the task but felt it was my responsibility and obligation.

With dread in the pit of my stomach, I went knocking on his bedroom door to charm him with good news like "Did I tell you that I got a hundred percent on a test?" It was an icebreaker, often preceded by hours, days, or maybe even weeks of my father walking in and out of his room, speaking to no one. The air was thick, at times even unbearable. Someone had to do something, and that someone was usually me.

When I was in his room, it typically meant a full hour of extreme self-discipline. I would stand and listen—or pretend to listen—as he rambled about a subject, like

Spinoza, that I found irrelevant and uninteresting. I'd stand there, my physical self at attention while my mental self escaped. He talked on and on; I daydreamed about my friends outside, wondering how long it would take before I was dismissed. He didn't care or didn't have the ability to see that I was uninterested. I desperately wanted to go out and play. He had captured me and was going to have my undivided attention. I was an imposter, but he had no sense of that. I was transformed into a "respectful, loving daughter," but I was resentful and distant. I hated him.

During these encounters in my father's room, I was not allowed to yawn. Yawning was an insult to him. On the rare occasion when I was no longer capable of swallowing it or when my clenched jaws could take it no longer, I would give in to a yawn.

With a disgusted look on his face, he would say with agitation, "You're yawning, right?" I knew I had failed, and I feared that the time I had already invested in the "happiness mission" would be for nothing. I was disappointed in myself for not having more self-control. I knew the rules of "the game." I stood until I was excused, overcome with a tremendous sense of relief. Oddly, the success of the mission also validated my sense of happiness. It was as though I had been given a certification of happiness for a few hours and, if I was really lucky, possibly even for a few days.

I called this validation the yo-yo effect. If my father was happy, then I was allowed to be happy; if he was down, he pulled me down with him, but it was within my power to bring him back up again. These interactions created a force beyond my comprehension and control, or so I believed. No matter how many times I told myself that I would not be pulled into his emotional fluctuations, I still was. I was often rewarded with my father's improved spirits, so I considered my mission accomplished, regardless of the cost to me.

After a while, I did not need to be prompted by my mother to go and entertain him. I knew that "Laci look," and I knew my calling. I knew how to perform my "tricks," and I had accepted my responsibility and self-appointed obligation to the clan.

Always anticipating the next conflict was exhausting. Our house was never a pleasant place to be. I remained on guard for the next attack, which fluctuated between fury and silence. A terrifying fight would seem to finish, but the fight would often be followed by what sometimes seemed even worse than the fight: my father's intense, dreaded silent treatment. For days, weeks, months, and what may even have been years, my father walked past my mother, my brother, and—in later years—my sister without uttering a single word. It was unbearable. We learned to handle conflict in this way. Fluctuations between anger and muteness became fairly common at home.

My brother, fortunately, had a sense of humor and was able to break the silence between us children. He joked until my sister and I had no choice but to start laughing and loosen the tension. For example, my brother believed he had exclusive rights over the only television we had, that is, excluding the one used for private viewing in my father's room. So, on a whim, my sister and I would be informed that *Combat* was on and that we should vanish. A fight would break out, and my sister and I would be left defeated and angry. Our anger didn't stop my brother from repeatedly banishing us from the television, but our silent treatment seemed to upset him, so he tried to penetrate us with humor.

"I have a question for you," he would say.

"What?" we would answer angrily.

"Are you not speaking to me?" he would ask with feigned innocence.

CHRISTMAS AND THE FUNKY BIKE

On several occasions during my childhood, my father tried to convince me that he was not Jewish and, therefore, I was not a Jew. He said he had converted to be a Hungarian Protestant and claimed he had the documents to prove it. I knew his statement was most likely, a lie. Years later, when he suffered a bout of depression and I managed his affairs, I found a document that had been written in Israel. It stated that he was a Christian. I doubt the authenticity of it, but it did bear the name of his best friend, Levi, as a witness. I think this was a sort of "Schutz pass" in his mind, the kind of fictitious document given to the Jews of Budapest, Hungary, during WWII by Raoul Wallenberg, a young Swedish diplomat, stating that these Hungarian Jews were under the protection of the Swedish government. Those fake documents given out at the Swedish embassy saved many lives.

He believed this certificate of Christianity could also save his life. He would be prepared for the next

Holocaust. Living in a non-Jewish neighborhood, I felt that this was my ticket in. I began to tell my friends that I was Protestant. After a while, however, saying those words didn't feel right. I was ashamed, so I stopped. I loved being Jewish. I loved everything Jewish around me: my mother, my relatives, the Jewish food, the old Jewish neighborhood.

But my father went on pretending that we were something we were not. It was a game, and I was forced to be a pawn. Or maybe it was his reality. I don't really know for sure. I dreaded the holidays because they were almost always a cause of conflict at home. My parents mostly chose to ignore the fact that these holidays existed. We celebrated nothing, not Chanukah, not Yom Kippur, not Rosh Hashanah, and not even Thanksgiving. The one holiday in which my father was willing to participate was Christmas. I knew that celebrating Christmas was wrong, and I wanted no part of it. It was hurtful to my mother, a slap in the face, and clearly meant to provoke her.

However, we longed to receive a gift for the holidays like all the other children in the neighborhood. In fact, just one would have been enough. We asked and asked until one day my father consented, but the gift would have to be on his terms, and the holiday celebration could not have any Jewish significance. I must have been around nine or ten years old the first time my father created his version of Christmas. It started with a small, tabletop Christmas tree, complete with tinsel and metallic balls. My father set it up on his desk in his room.

On Christmas Day, after his long preparations, he privately invited my sister and me into his room. Before we received our gift, we had to admire the decorated tree as he played "Silent Night" and other Christmas music on the record player. I felt sick and wanted it to end quickly. I knew this celebration was wrong, but it was this or nothing, so I chose to play along. How could I go out on Christmas Day in my Catholic neighborhood and report to my friends that I got nothing? It was unacceptable. I'm not sure whether I wanted the gift to satisfy my own wishes or to eliminate the embarrassment I would feel when I reported to the neighborhood girls.

My brother was excluded because by age fifteen, he had already stopped maneuvering through my father's obstacle course; they barely had contact with each other. Their communication, as with my father and my mother, was mostly through an interpreter: me. My brother got nothing. For obvious reasons, my mother was also excluded.

I can count on one hand the number of gifts we received over the years. First, there was the Baby Magic doll, which my sister and I shared. Later came the Instamatic camera for my birthday, of which my father still reminds me well into my forties; the child-sized record player that he often took away and kept locked in his room because Liz and I "didn't know how to properly care for it"; and the funky bike that we also shared.

In the late sixties, banana seat bicycles were "in," and every ten-year-old had to have one. Naturally, my sister and I asked for a banana seat bicycle. It was extremely unlikely that my father would consent, but for some odd reason, he agreed to buy us the bike for Christmas. In another family, this request would not have been unreasonable because we sisters, at the ages of nine and ten, did not own a bike. But he would only buy one bike, and we would have to share it. It was better than nothing, so we worked it out. My sister and I, excited about our forthcoming good fortune, ran to the bike store a few blocks away on the corner of Fort Hamilton Parkway and Sixty-ninth Street to eye the beauty that we would soon acquire. After a few minutes of debating the color, we chose the one we wanted—blue. I waited with bated breath for my father to announce that it was time to go and purchase it.

With excitement, I hurriedly walked with my father to the bicycle store. We walked in, and I scanned the room as we waited for the salesman to approach us. I spotted the cool, blue banana seat bicycle with the small frame, high handlebars, and thick wheels that I wanted and that I knew my sister had agreed on. My father immediately steered me away from it and over to what he referred to as the "very well-made English bike." I tried to explain that this was not really a "banana seat bike" and that although it was nice, it was not what we wanted. It was no use. He had made up his mind. What we wanted did not matter.

He called the storeowner over and asked him if he could put a banana seat and high handle bars on to this oversized, thin-wheeled Raleigh bicycle. The man, looking somewhat perplexed but wanting to make a sale, said he could. It was a deal. It was final: the oversized Raleigh or nothing. To my despair, the large, adult-sized Raleigh that had been transformed into a banana seat was coming home with us. I didn't know how to tell my sister the news. Our beauty had turned into an ugly duckling.

My sister and I didn't have to worry about sharing it because it was too much of an embarrassment to ride. Non-English-speaking Jews in a Christian neighborhood with immigrant parents who didn't sleep together and always fought didn't need to stick out any more than we already did, so we avoided the bicycle. We waited and hoped that one day we would be fortunate enough to acquire "the real thing."

After a year or two, another bicycle arrived. Surprise, surprise! It wasn't the "in," chunky-wheeled banana seat. It was a smaller, transformed, banana-seat version of the bigger, "well-made English," three-speed, thin-wheeled Raleigh. Once again, he had asked the man to change the seat and the handlebars. We settled for it because it could at least pass for the trendy, thick-wheeled "real banana seat."

In a addition to the few gifts, my sister, brother, and I received a weekly allowance, ranging from seventy-five cents when we were small to five dollars when we entered college. I had to sign for every dollar in my father's black marble composition book. I'll call that book "Number One" because there was a second black marble composition book for his health obsessions. In Number One, he meticulously logged every dime he ever gave us.

On Sunday nights, I was called into his room and told to sign on two separate lines of the book: one line for the weekly fifteen dollars he gave my mother and one for the combined eight dollars he gave my sister and I. Each Sunday night, I waited for him to call me to his room. "Keti, I am ready for you," he would say.

In his room, the entries were already prepared: *Weekly pay for mother* and *Allowance for Sheva and Kathy 5+3=8*. All that was left was for me to sign and make the deliveries. I felt violated. I knew that he was documenting everything he gave us— money for shoes, a dress, and even the dentist—but I couldn't understand why. I knew other fathers didn't do this. What did he have to prove? We were his family, not his business associates. Of what use could signatures for a few dollars be to him? I especially hated being used as the messenger between my mother and father. All this time they were only a few feet apart, yet it was always "Give your mother . . . ," "Tell your mother . . . ," or "Ask your mother . . . ."

In later years, my father would claim that Number One and its record of a few hundred dollars attested to the fact that he was a "loving, caring father." He often responded to accusations of his ineptitude by saying, "I loved all of you in the best possible way. I have the book with the hundreds of dollars to prove it." He lived in a world of fixed, false beliefs, but they were his reality.

My mother and the three of us children had our own methods for dealing with the stress. My brother acted out in anger, often breaking furniture. My sister threw tantrums. My mother occasionally became what my father called "hysterical." Those rare occasions when my mother broke down were very scary for me. I relied on her stability. She made me feel safe, and when she was out of control, I felt she was too vulnerable to my father—and to me. In some way, I feared the unimaginable: losing my mother.

On those rare occasions, usually after a fight with my father, my mother began to cry uncontrollably. My father led her, fully dressed, into the shower, where she stayed under the running water for a few minutes until she stopped crying. I watched from outside the bathroom, petrified. Fortunately, I don't remember this happening more than once or twice.

Between my brother breaking furniture, my sister throwing fits, my fragile mother crying, and my father fluctuating between bouts of anger and withdrawal, our household was in constant turmoil. Someone or something always erupted, and I always waited for the next outburst.

I had my own way of dealing with the stress. I didn't cry or act out in anger. I developed a repertoire for comforting myself in difficult times. For as long as I can remember, I sucked my thumb and simultaneously twirled my hair in my ear as I ran my toes through the comforter. Only then was I calm. I continued those habits well into my teens.

In my later teens, I discovered ways other than thumb sucking to soothe myself. While at City College, I began long-distance running. Running was a pleasurable outlet. It got me out of the house for hours in the evening, and I experienced the added benefit of the endorphin effect. Day after day, I ran for hours at a time.

In 1979, after running for a few years, I decided to try running my first New York City Marathon. Excitement was in the air. My brother, his friend Sonny, my sister, and our friends Rosanne Geraci and Lorraine McBride were as excited to watch me as I was to take on the challenge. We all prepared for the day. While I trained physically, they planned their strategy for viewing. They set it up so that they could travel the subways from Brooklyn and meet up with me at various points in Brooklyn and Manhattan along the route. The marathon would pass three blocks from my house, so I was sure that I would see my cheering committee there; anyplace else would be a bonus.

Aside from this group of loyal supporters, I also announced to my mother and my father that they did not have to travel far to see me on my special day because the race would pass only a few blocks from our home. We lived on Seventieth Street and Seventh Ave. Conveniently, the race would pass Seventieth Street and Third Ave. They simply had to walk four blocks to watch me capture my dream. The night before the race, I reminded my father about the marathon and where he could stand to see me. He never showed much excitement, but I was sure he understood the importance of the event to me.

The race started, and I was off to run 26.2 miles through the five boroughs of New York. We ran across the Verrazano Bridge to the first town over the bridge: Bay Ridge, Brooklyn, my hometown. I was elated, euphoric. It was a feeling that only one who runs a marathon can describe. The cheers and energy were beyond belief. Within a few miles, I spotted my sister, brother, and our friends along the way, snapping pictures and cheering me on. I reached Seventieth Street and Third Avenue, and there was my mother, rooting for me. Alone. I looked around, sure that my father was tucked somewhere amid the crowd. He was nowhere to be found. I suppressed the pain and continued the marathon, sure that there must have been some sort of misunderstanding. He surely understood the significance of the race to me. My spectators followed me to the finish line and helped me celebrate a day I will always remember.

When I reached home, I was exhausted and euphoric at the same time. As I walked toward his closed bedroom door, I gave him the benefit of the doubt: he must have simply screwed up and fallen back to sleep or forgotten the time. But this affair would turn out to be another disappointment, as were all the other important events of my childhood in which he did not participate. I took a deep breath and knocked on his door.

"It is me, Keti," I said as I opened the door.

He sat with disheveled hair and dirty long johns on his army cot. He looked up at me without any expression.

"Did you know that I was running the marathon today?" I asked.

"Yes," he said. "How was it?"

"Great. But I thought you were going to be there because it was so close to home. You did know that I passed only four blocks from home, right?"

The matter-of-fact look on his face spoke to me. He did not feel my distress.

"Yes," he answered. "I didn't sleep so well last night, so I was too tired."

I walked out. He didn't understand. I had always thought it was about my mother and their bad marriage. I had always thought that he didn't go to family events because he didn't want to be with my mother or with her family, but I realized at that moment that it was also about me. He couldn't bring himself to celebrate me.

DON'T GET SICK!

Rule 6: My father was always sick, but no one else dared to get sick; by no means was anyone else to infect him.

My father had a permanent appendage from his mouth: a thermometer. He checked his temperature at least once a day, and he watched for any minute fluctuation. If his temperature was a little low, it was a problem, and if it was a little high, it was equally a problem. He measured and measured, waiting for the next fluctuation. He was ready to act at any moment to prevent the deadly disease from happening. His drawers were full of defenses for potential ailments: antibiotics, analgesics, ointments, and creams. He harassed doctors until they gave him an overabundance of medications, which he then stored for later use. He was on constant surveillance against "catching a draft." In his Number Two black marble composition book, he meticulously recorded the symptoms he had experienced, the logistics of how he had managed the situation, his temperature, and how he should handle the symptoms if they were to recur. He spent hours on this self-monitoring. Here is an example:

January 25, 1997: *I got wounds on the top of my mouth and upper gum, where before I had a tooth. Maybe in the senior center they kissed me on my lips (what woman used to do in the Legion). These old slots [sluts] are practicing oral sex. So don't let them kiss my lips. It lasted about eight days. In my opinion, this will burn. I took half a cup of light warm tea with a teaspoon of salt and rinsed two to three times a day, then with peroxide.*

New entry: *Again wounds in top of mouth, especially the left gum where tooth 4/1/97 was extracted. Maybe I don't eat in senior center. I eat only canned soup and food. Lack of vitamins? I should cook chicken soup with "fresh" chicken and fresh vegetables and fruit? Theragran-M I bought made in China. Next time buy made in USA. Maybe when I have a bad cold, I don't get terramycin injection and I don't use up 400 mg erythromycin for whole ten days? I should clean denture plate after every meal with baking soda. Maybe instead of 500 mg time delay capsules, I should take 400 mg liquid erythromycin every four hours for ten days.*

New entry: *The fungus comes from dirt underneath the nail. Remove this dirt with water and soap. Brush strongly this corner, especially the opening, and brush every fingernail.*

New entry: *Maybe during dancing I got the "fungus" from holding the slot's [slut's] hand. After dancing, right away wash hands with soap! My suggestion on 7/4/2000! Before and after dancing, take one erythromycin capsule with food, and wash mouth and teeth with Listerine + baking soda + peroxide before and after dancing. Wash teeth and gurgle [gargle] every day, and don't eat without partial plate, not even one bite.*

Rule 6 Revisited: We were not to get sick. Getting sick was a failure.

If I got sick, then I had messed with the system. For the most part, my illnesses were routine childhood colds and needing to go to the dentist. We prayed not to get a cold. If we did get a cold, we also got the "Laci look." My father would be extra annoyed and angry with us, as though we had done something wrong. In his mind, we had: we posed a threat to his well-being. We tried desperately to hide the evidence. In the earlier years, if we were found out, it was simple. He would call the doctor to come to our home to give each of us a shot of penicillin. Later, however, as shots were no longer the norm and house calls a thing of the past, that strategy became more difficult.

We tried to conceal our colds the best we could. Coughing was prohibited. Trying to conceal the cough during the day while my father was at work was not too hard. But at night, when coughs often get worse, he was in his bedroom right next door; we were doomed. Each time my sister and I had the urge to cough, we covered our faces with our pillows to muffle the sound. Sooner or later, he heard the cough, and we immediately heard the click of his bedroom door opening. As he stood on the other side of our door and turned the knob to our room, my sister and I looked at each other. Our eyes said, "Uh-oh! Daddy's coming!" As he opened our door, we froze.

"Who was coughing?" he asked angrily.

My sister and I exchanged looks until one of us reluctantly admitted to the cough.

He would stand at the doorway with accusations as to how we had brought this upon ourselves. According to him, we had caused this, done something wrong, or should have done something to prevent it. "You went out half naked, and that's why you are sick," he would say. The dentist was another story. I should say *dentists* because there were so many of them that I lost track after a while. We had a new dentist every year or two depending on how often we had to go. My father didn't trust any of them, and we were always switching to "the new great dentist" because the old one was allegedly a "shoemaker" or a "crook." As much as possible, my sister and I avoided our dental care so that we didn't have to face the dilemma. Fortunately, my brother had perfect teeth and never required a dentist. When we were somewhere around fourteen or fifteen, my sister and I found our own dentist through a friend and had some consistency from that point on, but that process was not easy either because my father was never willing to pay without extensive explanation. Asking to have dental work done meant getting the "Laci look." Dental work often required several appointments, so each time we needed to go back, we had to go through the same ordeal. No one wanted to face the "Laci look" and allegations of failing the system, so my sister and I devised our own system that required no direct contact or dialogue with him.

Our system went like this: We waited until after 10:00 p.m. when we were sure that he was asleep. Then, we wrote a note addressed to *Dear Daddy* to butter him up, asking for the amount needed and explaining what we needed it for. It ended with *Love, Kathy* or *Love, Liz.* After we heard the door click inside his room and the key turn, we knew that he had now locked himself in— and us out—for the night. We knew that it was time to mobilize the operation. We discreetly placed the note in front of his door so that when he woke up to get ready for work at the local crane factory where he worked as a machinist, he would see it. After strategically placing the note, we prayed that he wouldn't need to use the toilet before we had a chance to fall asleep. If he did, we'd pretend to be asleep to avoid interrogation. This system usually worked, and most of the time the money we needed for our dental work was placed on the dining room table. All that remained was the task of signing his Number One composition book when he got home.

As difficult as those situations were, the incident that most vividly stays with me is the day we became United States citizens. I was sixteen. On November 6, 1974, my father, my sister, and I were going to become United States citizens. Although we had qualified years earlier, the new impetus was that we were to begin classes, which were a lot cheaper for U.S. citizens, at the City University of New York system. My brother refused to go. He was already at the City College of New York; what did he care if my father had to pay a higher price? My brother knew the importance of education to my father, and he was certain it was something my father was not willing to sabotage. My mother was excluded because my father did not want to help her become a U.S. citizen. She would have to figure that out on her own. Off we went to the courtroom. The event was scheduled to take three hours.

A few minutes after the start of the ceremony, I began to have pains in my abdomen. The pain grew worse with each passing moment. At first, I tried to shift positions and do what I could to ease the pain. Within minutes, it became so intense that I could think of nothing else but the throbbing inside of me. I sat, wringing my hands. When that no longer worked, I twisted my feet as I obediently sat, not uttering a word. I prayed that the ceremony would end.

The room was quiet; with only ceremonial speakers giving lengthy lectures about the privilege and honor it was to be a U.S. citizen. The soon-to-be citizens were called up one by one and asked questions about the Constitution, the country's history, and other subjects they had studied in preparation to prove their worthiness for citizenship. I looked around the large room and could not believe how many people would be called up to the judge. I didn't know how I would make it through the never-ending event. I sat petrified that I would be called up because there was no way I could stand. I sat and prayed and wished and hoped that I would not be called upon. I prayed that I would not cry or yelp in pain. I prayed that I would be able to conceal what was happening so that I would not upset my father or his plans for the day.

Minutes felt like hours, and when I could no longer bear the pain, I leaned over to my sister and whispered that I was having excruciating pain. My sister was not as intimidated by my father as I was. She told him of my pain. He barely reacted. There was no choice. We came here to become citizens, and we would leave here as citizens, which meant waiting until the very end when they would award us our certificates.

Finally, the ceremony was over, and I began crying, begging my father to get me to a doctor as fast as possible. My father hailed a cab, which was in itself completely out of character, and the three of us went to Dr. Romm's antiquated office. I had never been to him before and had no idea who he was, but I didn't care. The plaque on his door said M.D. He was a decrepit man who seemed to be at least eighty years old. He was my father's "chosen" doctor for the year. Like the dentists, my father was always finding "the best doctor." Dr. Romm charged three dollars; that was the reason he was selected. Fortunately, Dr. Romm knew enough to send me straight to Maimonides Medical Center's emergency room. An emergency appendectomy was performed that night even though the need for the appendectomy was inconclusive. The doctors were not convinced of the diagnosis, but because it was a probable appendicitis, my appendix was removed.

Within a few days, I recovered from the surgery and was ready to be discharged. There was only one problem: I didn't want to go home. My stay in the hospital was the first time I had been out of my house for any length of time since that nightmarish weekend at my friend Renee's house when I was twelve. I liked it. It was a respite, a real sense of calm that I had never experienced before.

People cared for me instead of me caring for them. I got attention instead of going unnoticed. At home, everyone else demanded so much attention.

Reluctantly, I returned home, wishing that I could be sick again. I thought, *What if they made a mistake?* I didn't just think it; I wished it. I wished that there would be something more. Within four weeks, the excruciating pain recurred. Back to the surgeon we went.

"It must be an infection from the appendectomy," the surgeon announced.

It was my lucky day. Back to the hospital I would have to go for a week's course of intravenous antibiotics. Without a moment's hesitation, I donned my hospital gown and climbed into my hospital bed for a week of relaxation. After the week of antibiotics, I was again ready to be released. Home I went, wishing that after I checked on how things were with the family for a few days, some physical condition left unsolved would earn me a subsequent admission to the hospital. To my disbelief, two days later, the attack recurred with more force and fury than I had experienced previously. This time, it scared me.

Occasionally, my father surprisingly did the sensible thing.

"Enough of Maimonides Medical Center! Dr. E. [the surgeon] is a crook and a shoemaker," he announced.

Where did the Hungarian Jews of Brooklyn go when Maimonides failed? Off I went to Mount Sinai Medical

Center in Manhattan for another glorious two-and-a-half-week hospital stay.

Something was wrong, very wrong. Was it my intestines? Was it my ovaries? Was it cancer? I had CT scans, upper GI's, lower GI's, gynecological tests, and even a horrifying bone marrow aspiration. All the while, I continued to have excruciating attacks of pain. Added to my vacation away from home, I was given demerol or morphine as needed around the clock. It was an injection in my thigh, so I waited until the pain became unbearable before I asked for it. Soon after each injection, I felt as if I were being lifted from the bed and placed on a floating cloud. It was the most peaceful calm I could have imagined.

After a week of the tests and no real answers, the pediatric surgeon, Dr. K., decided it was time to go in and have a look.

"She needs an exploratory laparotomy," he announced.

An exploratory laparotomy happens when they don't really know what's wrong, so they open you up, hoping to find the source of the problem. The surgeon found a duplication of my cecum with a cyst the size of a grapefruit. I had a resection to remove the cyst, and I spent another week in the hospital recovering before I reluctantly returned home.

I told myself, *OK, no more hospitals. No more wishing. You are going to have to figure out a different way to escape the hellhole.*

FAMILY PHOTOS

Our home had few pictures on the walls. A very large, golden-framed black-and-white photograph of my mother and father, taken shortly after their marriage, hung in the dining room. They looked happy in the picture. At times, the photograph was taken down, but I don't recall by whom. No other pictures were on display anywhere in our house except in my father's room. Not one picture of us children in the entire rest of the house. No pictures of relatives. In my father's room, he hung pictures of himself and the one of me and my sister on Easter, with my sister blocked out.

My mother had a few pictures of her family that she kept out of sight. She kept one particular photograph hidden in the dining room china cabinet between neatly stacked tablecloths. It was a picture of her sister Boreshka, the one who perished after being separated from my mother and her sister Reli during the last days of the war. Every once in a while, I would search for the picture and take it out for a look. I felt connected to Boreshka, as though she were part of the family and simply existed elsewhere. She was part of our family, and that was my visit with her. My mother loved Boreshka deeply, and looking at that picture always made my mother teary-eyed. Not until I was much older did I understand the depth of her emotion and guilt. My mother carried the burden of betraying Boreshka in her final days as well as the guilt of possibly contributing to her death by not watching over her. My mother didn't have a choice, yet she was tormented by her actions. I couldn't imagine what she was feeling and didn't know how to ease her pain.

Because I never saw them, I was convinced that my father did not have any pictures of his family. I later learned that he did have photos, but they were too painful for him to look at, so he kept them hidden. Occasionally, he took out a picture of his mother. I would walk into his room and find a framed picture facing the wall. The photograph was of his mother, and facing the wall was the only way he ever displayed her. His anguish over his family's demise was overwhelming. My father would often repeat how he was the only survivor of his family. "More than sixty members of my family perished in the Holocaust. Imagine, I am the only survivor of my entire family," he would say.

This statement was almost the truth. My father had contact with four relatives on a few occasions, and all those encounters occurred before I was seven or eight years old. He had two first cousins in Boro Park who were "too religious," according to my father; a cousin from Caracas, Venezuela, who came to our house once; and an Uncle Villi, who survived the Holocaust, lived in Canada, and visited us in Israel when I was too young to remember. That is the sum total of the contact we had with my father's family: four people on three or four occasions.

My mother, Israel, 1947

My Father-Israel, 1947

Liz, Me, My mother, Michael, Israel, 1960

Nursery school, Petah Tikva, Israel, Liz- bottom row, first from left, Me second row, forth from left, 1961

The Jerusalem-Our ship to America, 1963

Me (right) and Julie Shapiro a few months after arriving in America, Boro Park, Brooklyn, 1963

My brother Michael's Bar Mitzvah, Boro Park, Brooklyn, 1964

Me (left), Liz, Mom and Uncle Jeno in Williamsburg,
Brooklyn, 1966

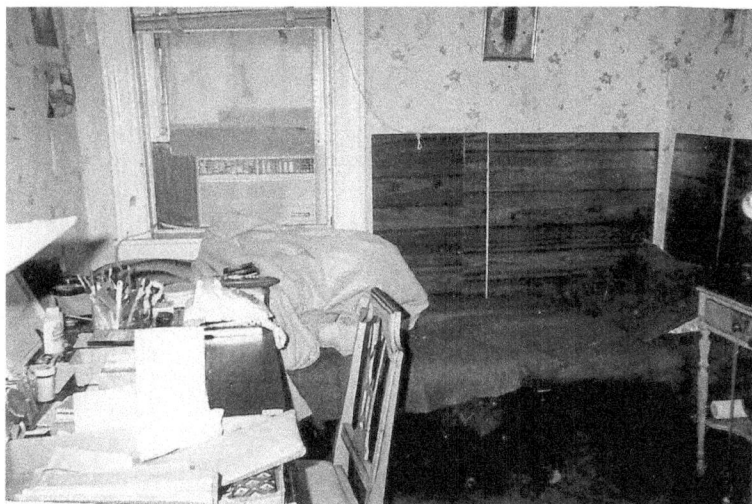

My Father's bedroom, Bay Ridge, Brooklyn, 1980

Christmas at Renee's, (L to R) Liz, Renee, Gail,
Irene and Me, Bay Ridge, 1967.

Me (right) and Liz with the funky bikes, 1969

Book Number One

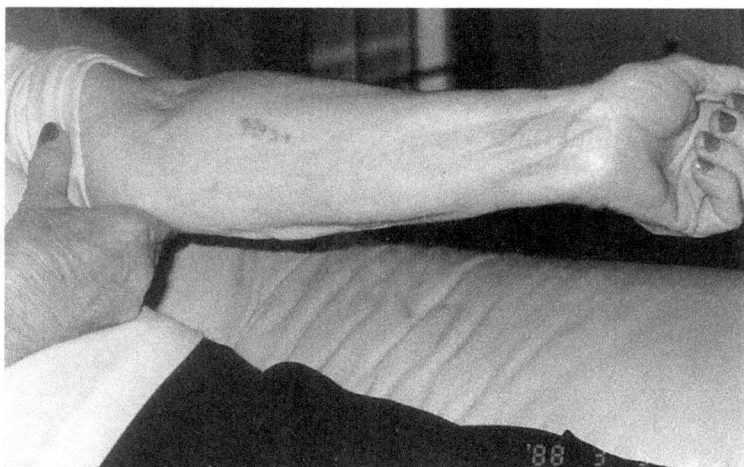

My mother, Auschwitz number A-12636

Me and my mother, Holocaust Convention Philadelphia, 1985

Me and My father-1993

Adam, Gary, Me, David and Jonathan 2011

MY MOTHER'S ILLNESS

After my experience as a hospital patient, I decided that I had a passion for medicine and would become what girls from my part of Brooklyn became: a nurse. My father had plans, or so he has said, for me to become a nurse. But his plans were different from mine. He planned for me to become a nurse and move into the upstairs apartment so that I could take care of him, and we, meaning he and I, could live happily ever after. It never occurred to him that I could—and would—have other plans.

I attended nursing school because I chose to. In my father's delusion, he believed that he had chosen it for me. One of the required courses in nursing school was a physical assessment class in which we learned to conduct complete physical exams. Each week, I practiced my newly acquired skill on my cooperative mother. We learned breast exams, so I came home and went right to work on my mother's breast exam. As soon as she undressed, she disclosed that she had noted a lump the size of a walnut in her left breast. I was shocked.

My father called around and made my mother an appointment to see a breast surgeon at Mount Sinai Medical Center. She would need to have a biopsy, and if the lump was determined to be malignant, she would immediately undergo a mastectomy. Over the years, my mother had bought brand new boxed nightgowns to be keep for a later date when she would have to go to the hospital. My mother now prepared to enter the hospital with the nightgowns she had saved, anticipating the day she would go to the hospital as though it was only a matter of time.

Her surgery was planned for the next morning. So was the New York City transit strike. Both went on as scheduled. My sister and I tried to figure out how we would get to Mount Sinai Hospital from Brooklyn to be at our mother's side when she awakened. Because it was at least fifteen miles away, we asked my father to go with us by car service, but he declined. I wondered what my mother would think when she woke up and saw that he wasn't there. But she knew him and his ways.

We thought we could take a car service or find a cab, but because everyone else was doing the same thing and drivers were reluctant to enter Manhattan altogether, we couldn't find a ride. We set out on foot and walked through Brooklyn, across the Brooklyn Bridge, and through most of Manhattan. After about four and a half hours, we reached Mount Sinai Hospital. My sister, twenty-one, and I, twenty, were greeted by my mother's surgeon.

"Where is your father?" he asked.

We excused our father by saying he couldn't make the journey because of the transit strike. We knew and the doctor knew that what he was about to say should be heard by a spouse, not by two young women barely out of their teens.

"Your mother has breast cancer," he said.

My sister and I began to cry. He might just as well have said, "Your mother is going to die" because that's what we heard. We had watched my mother's two sisters die of breast cancer in their early fifties, younger than my mother was. It was what we knew. Young women in my mother's family died of breast cancer. With surgeon-like stoicism, the doctor proceeded with the details of the operation, but he left us with the only words we heard: *your mother has breast cancer.*

The next day, as the transit strike continued, my cousin Yutka, despite the years of harassment and rejection she had received from my father, offered him, Liz, and me a ride to see my mother in the hospital. My father refused the offer. For no reason in the world would he get into her car. He despised her, along with all the other relatives, and no circumstance could force him to interact with them. I am unsure whether he ever visited my mother during her hospital stay.

Shortly after the operation and upon her return home to Brooklyn, I visited my mother. She asked me to go for a walk with her. She said she had something to tell me. I thought, *What now, God? I can't handle any more bad news.*

"I'm really five years older than you think," she said.

She wasn't sixty, but sixty-five. I was relieved that she wasn't sick or dying. Nonetheless, it was a bit of a surprise. My first thought was that she could die sooner than I had anticipated. But it made sense. She looked older than the other mothers because she was older. She was forty when I was born. I asked her who knew about her real age. She explained that she had recently told my brother but not yet my sister and that her cousins also knew because they had grown up with her in Hungary.

My mother went on to say that after the Holocaust, many of the survivors who wanted to immigrate to Israel lied about their age. They felt that they had a better chance of being accepted and helped by the Zionist movements if they were youthful.

"Does Daddy know?" I asked.

"No," she said.

My first thought was *Gee, I sure hope she's not counting on me to tell him because this is one mission I definitely do not want to take on.* He didn't like her much to start with. I didn't need to add fuel to the fire. To my relief, she indicated that she didn't want him to know.

My mother continued, "I thought he knew. We were set up in Israel by my cousin, Sanyi, and his miserable wife, Moti, who was also Daddy's cousin. I was sure Sanyi told Daddy my real age, but Daddy said something about my age one day, and I realized he didn't know the truth. With the way he was, I thought it best not to tell him. I didn't know how he would react."

Good thinking, I thought. Nothing to argue about here. She was absolutely right. Nothing good could possibly have come from telling him the truth. He would have used her age against her the first opportunity he got. He was never told.

ON MY OWN

After graduating from nursing school in 1980, I spent three months in Israel on a kibbutz. It had been a dream of mine for a long time, and it was finally becoming a reality. I had worked as a nurse's aide during nursing school to earn the money for the trip. As the departure date drew closer, I realized that I was short five hundred dollars. Though my father didn't want me to go, he agreed to lend me the money. We agreed that I would pay him back as soon as I returned and started my job at Mount Sinai Hospital the following September.

Seeds of skepticism had been planted in me through my father's anti-Jewish, anti-Zionist training, but I still wanted to go. My father taught me that Israel was "the most dangerous place in the world." According to him, he had succeeded in getting us out of that danger zone by a miracle. I was ready to go, but he became agitated and declared that he was not going to lend me the money. My mother dipped into her savings and came to my rescue. Shortly before I left, my father reversed his position and said he would give me the money.

"No, thanks," I said. "I already have it."

For the first time, I felt empowered. The financial hold he had exerted on me throughout my childhood began to weaken. I can only imagine how he felt as he realized he was no longer in control.

When the El Al jet landed at Ben-Gurion Airport and Hatikva, the Israeli national anthem played on the loudspeaker. I cried. I wanted to get out and kiss the ground. After fifteen years, I was back to the place of my birth, the place I had dreamt of for so long. It was one of the happiest days of my life.

I loved Israel. I was sent to Kibbutz Ma'agan on the Sea of Galilee, founded and inhabited by Hungarian Holocaust survivors. I felt that I was home for the first time in my life. The other kibbutz residents were Hungarian, nonreligious children of Holocaust survivors who welcomed me as one of their own. It was as though I had found my family, and it was big—really big. My summer on the kibbutz was one of the most rewarding periods of my life, but it was short-lived. I was expected to return home shortly "or else," although I didn't quite know what the "or else" would be. I knew that staying in Israel longer was not an option.

On the kibbutz, I spent days working and evenings socializing in the "kibbutznik" homes. Because I was an Israeli-born, somewhat-Hebrew-speaking, Hungarian child of Holocaust survivors, I was given work privileges not often given to foreign volunteers. I was allowed to work at the coffee shop, which was down the road and outside the kibbutz grounds. I helped make Israeli specialties like baba ganoush, a Middle Eastern eggplant salad, and I served the customers, most of whom were Israeli soldiers who stopped by the busload to eat. I was even allowed to handle the cash, which was a statement of trust. I loved the co-operative work and play. It was like being at camp or college, neither of which I had ever been allowed to experience.

My other jobs were tough but fun. I spent days picking grapes at 4:00 a.m. We were awakened early, boarded a tractor-pulled wagon, and pulled uphill to the vineyards where we crouched for hours under the triangular vines, clippers in hand, to carefully pick the grapes. Around 7:00 a.m., we rested and ate our Israeli-style breakfast at a picnic bench. We enjoyed fresh vegetables, hard-boiled eggs, cheese, yogurt, and coffee. We had worked up an appetite, and it all tasted so good. By 11:00 a.m., we were done and had the rest of the day to play at the Sea of Galilee, known as the Kinneret.

My least favorite job was kitchen duty. In the dining room, I spent hours scrubbing stainless steel table legs and napkin holders until they shone to the satisfaction of the kitchen leader. She was tough and not easy to please. Her daughter, Nilli, was one of my best friends on the kibbutz, which didn't seem to matter because her mother was still not nice to me. One of the advantages to kitchen duty, however, was that I learned how to make fried eggs for two hundred people at a time.

On the kibbutz, we were given work clothes, which included high-top work boots, khaki short shorts, and a dark blue shirt. We were also given a small amount of money and cigarettes. A small general store supplied food items, clothes, and other small items for purchase. I loved wearing the uniform; it gave me a sense of belonging. Being Hungarian and speaking Hebrew, I especially felt that I belonged because I was accepted by both the kibbutzniks and the volunteers. Most of the volunteers were from England, Australia, South Africa, and the United States. Volunteers were given one day off a week. We could take our day weekly, or we could accrue them and take them all at once. I saved all my days off for eight weeks and then left the kibbutz by myself to tour Israel for the first time.

I boarded a bus from Tiberius to Tel Aviv, where I spent the first night with my mother's best friend and my old babysitter, Ester. From there, I headed to a youth hostel in Jerusalem. I met two young men, one from South Africa and the other from Australia, who were also traveling on their own. We decided to travel the rest of the week together. We went to Jaffa, the Dead Sea, and Eilat. The last day of my journey, I was to meet up with my kibbutznik boyfriend, Avi Serussi, in the Negev at a place on the beach south of Eilat called Nuweiba. At the time, Nuweiba belonged to Israel. Today, it is part of Egypt.

Avi and I swam in the ocean and then placed our blankets on the sand, where we slept for the night. In the morning, we were awakened by Bedouins, desert inhabitants riding camels and selling us homemade pita bread for breakfast. The bread was delicious, spiced with salt air and a few grains of sand.

In September 1980, after spending three wonderful months in Israel, I returned home. I worked as a pediatric nurse at Mount Sinai Hospital in New York and rented an apartment. I was on my own, out of the misery.

Our home had grown a little calmer; my sister had moved to California, and my father desperately tried to get my brother to move out of the house. My mother resisted. She was particularly fond and defensive of my brother. Perhaps she felt guilty for denying him a proper father. On many occasions, despite the fact that I had moved out, I was summoned by my father to coerce my brother who was still living in the finished basement after he had finished college and had a well paying job, to move out. My mother was heartbroken. She tried to get along with my father, but she simply couldn't forgive him for wanting to throw their only son out of the house. One day, my brother finally had enough and moved to California, too.

My parents got along better by themselves, or so it seemed. It wasn't good; it was just better. My father took up ballroom dancing. He frequented Roseland and whatever other dance place he could find, and he stayed there until the early hours of the morning. He dressed in his sports jacket and tarnished silver necklace, dancing the night away, leaving my mother behind.

The inevitable happened. He had a lady—or ladies. There were at least two, but I am quite certain there were more. One day, I got a call from my mother. She said my father had confessed to her that he was having an affair. My mother wanted to know what she should do. I wasn't surprised. Well, actually, I was surprised that anyone would want him. My mother told me he was seeing an Italian woman named Rose, and the reason my father had told my mother was because he wanted to end the affair, but Rose was not making it easy for him. Rose had threatened to tell his wife and family. Rose had also warned my father that if he left her, he would have to worry about the retaliation of her Italian family. This threat was the real source of my father's fear.

The woman began to call my mother and even followed her to the supermarket once, intercepting her in the checkout line. She told my mother about my father and their relationship. Because my mother did not speak or understand much English, the woman must have been dissatisfied with her interactions with my mother. Rose began to call me on the telephone. She told me she was in a relationship with my father and that my father assured her she wouldn't have to worry about my mother interfering because my mother had breast cancer and would probably die in a few years. I didn't doubt this story for a second. My father would think nothing of saying those words.

His cruelty had no limits. My mother walked with

a limp because she had a congenitally dislocated hip. My father often claimed that she had hidden the limp from him and that he had been unaware of it when he married her. "How do you hide a limp?" my mother would say. "What am I? A flamingo that can stand around, hiding my leg under my wing?" His words hurt her, but she became immune to his heartlessness—or at least pretended to for my sake.

LEVI WEISS

Not long after I began working at Mount Sinai, I heard that my father's best friend from Israel, Levi Weiss, was here in America being treated for liver cancer at the same hospital. He and my father had been through a great deal together. They had been together in the army hospital in Hungary. They had remained close friends in Israel. My father made arrangements to meet him and his wife for dinner at the most expensive Chinese restaurant in Manhattan. My mother was not invited. He wanted to take Levi and his wife to Roseland for dancing after dinner. Not surprisingly, they declined, so he dropped them off at their hotel room and went to Roseland by himself.

Levi returned to Israel, then came back some months later to be treated at Mount Sinai again. This time, he was gravely ill. Although he and his wife fiercely resisted giving up their hope of finding a curative treatment for his metastatic disease, Levi was losing the fight and dying.

Levi's wife, Hana, called the house to tell my father of Levi's dire situation. My father wished him well, and that was the end of it for him. My mother could not believe that my father had refused to visit his best friend who needed him as he lay dying. Distraught, my mother telephoned me. What could she do? How could my father show such indifference? I told my mother that we would go to see Levi without my father. The next day, I met my mother in front of Levi's room. My mother and I looked at each other and took a deep breath before we could find the courage to walk in. Levi's wife was sitting at the edge of his hospital bed, and there in the bed was Levi, emaciated from his illness. He was a sweet, good-looking man despite the graveness of his prognosis. I had met him years earlier when I was a child in Israel, but I remembered him mostly from photographs.

Levi was delighted that we had come to see him. He scanned the room.

"Where's Laci?" he asked.

My mother tried to explain, saying that Levi knew my father and his ways. She told him how she had tried to get him to come with her. I watched the expression on Levi's face change from joy to sadness.

Levi lay quietly as tears rolled down his gaunt face. I knew his disappointment. It was a familiar part of my life. I wanted to reach out to him, but I hardly knew him. My heart ached, and I now hated my father more than I had ever hated him before. My father didn't deserve a friend.

Levi soon went back to Israel because there were no more treatments to offer him. He died a few weeks later.

GARY

When I was twenty-six, I met my husband, Gary. We were set up on a blind date by a pediatrician I worked with named Harold Raucher. He was Gary's basketball teammate. It was my first blind date, and I was skeptical. Gary arrived in an outdated, three-piece suit. Something in him or me made me give him a chance anyway. We went to an Italian restaurant named Parma on Third Avenue and Seventy-ninth Street. We talked easily with each other, and the conversation took interesting turns. He was good looking, had a nice body, and owned a nice car. I especially liked the space between his front teeth.

As we talked over our dinner, the Holocaust made its way into our conversation. Gary's Aunt Susan had been killed in the Holocaust, and his mother had survived by hiding in Amsterdam. As he told his story, I felt a magnetic pull. He would understand. He met my most stringent criterion for a successful, long-term relationship. We talked for hours, he paid the bill, and we walked to his car. We arrived at the parking garage, but Gary couldn't find the parking ticket. He searched deep into every pocket until it finally appeared. I saw the lost ticket, but what registered with me was that he had remained calm. He had passed the second test: no anger, no agitation. I was trained to read emotions, and I felt tension whenever something went wrong. I waited for the look that said "Uh-oh! Trouble ahead. Beware: anger, guilt, tension. Be prepared." But Gary's calm drew me to him.

On our next date, we went to Fort Lee, New Jersey, where Gary lived. As Gary was driving me back to my apartment in New York, we got into an accident on the George Washington Bridge. I watched Gary walk away from his damaged BMW with a smile and barely a grimace. I said to myself, *OK, this guy is for me.*

The risk of meeting someone on a blind date is that you meet in artificial territory. The matchmaker didn't know much about my background or didn't care. Gary, unlike me, was raised in an upper-middle-class, Jewish, suburban home in Englewood Cliffs, New Jersey. I really liked him, but I wondered whether this relationship could, would, or should work out. As we continued to date, I knew the inevitable would happen. We would meet each other's families. Our families were very different.

I prepared my father. I bought him a new, light blue shirt to wear instead of his twenty-year-old, dark blue, factory-stenched, obsessively worn shirt. I pleaded with him to promise me one thing above all: positively, absolutely, under no condition was he ever to let Gary see his bedroom. He was not even to leave the door open for a split second. I was utterly embarrassed by what Gary would see: the army cot, clotheslines, flypaper, oven grills, washbasins, dirty floral wallpaper.

During the first few encounters, my father abided by the rules. But after those first few visits, my father began to feel more comfortable and began to relax. First, he left the door ajar. Eventually, he left it open. Each time I came into my parents' house with Gary, I dashed to the back of the house for the routine inspection to make sure that my father's bedroom door was closed.

Occasionally, when I found the door open, I would turn to my father and say, "You promised me you would keep your bedroom door closed."

He would give me a mischievous smile and respond, "Don't worry."

I had the feeling that he would be satisfied if he sabotaged my relationship with Gary.

One day, I let my guard down and didn't check that all systems were clear. After we entered the house, I stayed in the living room to talk to my mother as Gary went to the bathroom. Within moments, I realized the danger, but it was too late. I darted to my father's bedroom. Gary stood in my father's room along with my father, who wore a defiant look. My father showed Gary the things in his room, and I was convinced that this was a perfectly executed plan. I was exposed.

When we left, I apologized to Gary and wanted to explain to him who my father was, though I knew the truth was obvious from what Gary had uncovered. Gary kept saying that he didn't notice anything wrong. "His room wasn't so bad," he said reassuringly. I was grateful and full of admiration that Gary knew what to say and knew not to humiliate me more than I already was.

When I met Gary's family, I wasn't sure how his parents would handle our differences. They were kind, nonjudgmental, and accepting. Gary and I got engaged after about a year of getting to know each other. Now, our parent's would have to meet. My father could present himself well because he was intelligent. Despite his awkwardness, he was a scholarly, refined man who had obviously grown up cultured. He was articulate and well versed in many topics. As long as he let me pick out his clothes, which, of course, I purchased for the occasion, he could camouflage as "normal." I was more concerned about my mother, who could not converse in English. And although it is difficult for me to admit that I cared, she limped. Despite all my fear, the initial encounter went well.

The wedding was planned for March 27, 1987. As the day drew near, my father grew resistant. "If you seat me near Molvin [my mother's sister], then I won't come," he threatened. He had the potential to not show up, as he had done so many times before for so many special occasions. Until the wedding day, I wondered if he would pull out. I imagined the humiliation of not having my father walk me down the aisle. This one time, he came through.

MY PREMONITION

During my early teen years, I had a premonition that I would not live past the age of thirty. I didn't imagine illness or a catastrophic event; I just couldn't envision my life beyond thirty.

On October 4, 1988, my first son, Adam, was born. It was the moment I had dreamt of. I had a child at last! But my joy turned bittersweet: Adam was born three and a half weeks before I was to turn thirty.

The due date came and went with no signs of labor. Exactly two weeks after my due date, I was scheduled for an induction. After epidurals, pitocin, and a few hours of induction, the baby's heart rate dipped dramatically, and the doctor decided there was no choice but to do an emergency C-section. The verdict: dry birth, no amniotic fluid.

I remember Adam in the delivery room as I lay there, flying high from medications. That was the last time I saw almost anything clearly for several days. I entered what I call a "near-death black zone."

When I arrived at the hospital, I had mentioned to the doctors my allergy to penicillin. With the emergency C-section, they gave me a prophylactic, intravenous antibiotic from a class of drugs called cephalosporins. Around 3:00 or 4:00 a.m. on the night of Adam's birth, I woke in panic, gasping for air. I tried to wake Gary, who was sleeping on the cot next to me. With my newly acquired abdominal stitches, I got on my hands and knees and begged my husband to call for help.

"I can't breathe," I said.

"What do you mean you can't breathe?" Gary asked.

"My uvula is swollen. Please, please," I pleaded. "Get the doctor fast."

The uvula is the little thing that hangs like a pendulum in the back of your throat. Every time I took a breath, I felt like I was inhaling it. It blocked my airway at the back of my throat.

Gary ran from the room and returned within a few minutes with a very groggy resident who was not pleased at being awakened at 4:00 a.m. I tried to explain how I was feeling as she took her time checking my breathing.

I kept saying, "Get me oxygen, Benadryl, Solu-Cortef, please. I beg you. I can't breathe. Please I beg you," I repeated.

Aggravated, the young doctor looked at me and said, "If you can talk, you can breathe" as she walked out of the room.

I was lightheaded; I felt I was going to lose consciousness. I thought, *God, why did you leave me to die in the hands of a moron?* Within a few minutes that felt like hours to me, she returned with an oxygen tank in tow.

In my panic, I persisted, "The steroid, please, please. I think I am having an allergic reaction."

She rolled her eyes with an expression that said, "Oh yeah, right. You're one of those know-it-all nurses." Then, she walked away. I donned the oxygen but felt doomed.

Within seconds, I was in total darkness. Everything around me was a black nothingness, and I was its core. My vision was reduced to a pinhole. I struggled to see through it, and I panicked that this minute window would close. From a position somewhere above my bed, I watched as I tried to get out of the imaginary black coffin in which I had been placed. I was paralyzed, and all I could do was wish that the light would come back and release me from deathly darkness.

I lay desperate and helpless in that coffin. Someone brought my baby in, and I kept thinking, *I can't see. I wish I could see him.* I tried to maneuver my body so that he would come into focus, but I couldn't. I could not get out of the darkness. After several hours, the darkness slowly lifted, but I had been placed in some other zone—a zone of panic and fear.

I knew the nursing supervisor on the maternity floor. She came into my room sometime around 8:00 a.m., a few hours after the ordeal had started, to see what was happening. I begged her to call one of the doctors from otolaryngology to examine me. I will be forever grateful to her and to the doctor who confirmed that I had an allergic reaction to the antibiotic, which had caused my uvula to enlarge and obstruct my airway. I was immediately put on steroids and kept on oxygen for the next few days. I later learned that a certain percentage of people who are allergic to penicillin are also allergic to cephalosporins, the class of antibiotics they had given me in the delivery room. Little by little, I emerged from the darkness, but that event continued to haunt me.

When Adam was six months old, I returned to work at Mount Sinai and weaned him from breast-feeding. Shortly after I stopped breast-feeding, I experienced postpartum depression. One day, when Adam was barely able to stand in his playpen, panic struck.

I had prepared a dinner of red snapper. My mother was visiting. As my husband, mother, and I sat at the dining room table, I suddenly felt flushed. Lightheadedness soon followed, and within minutes, I was convinced that like the time in the hospital, I was having an allergic reaction to the fish. I told my husband to call an ambulance. After the episode in the hospital, he had pledged to call for help immediately if I should ever need it. The paramedics arrived, gave me oxygen, and carried me down four flights of steps. I passed my small son, who looked at me curiously as strangers carried me out on a board, and I passed my mother, who was paler than I was. I hated to have her witness that moment.

We reached the hospital, and no one said much of anything. The emergency room staff believed my attack was caused by anxiety. They didn't say it overtly, and I didn't ask too much. When I felt better, I got up and we returned home with the assurance that Gary would stand by me and call for help again if I ever needed or wanted him to. Fortunately, that was the only time. Over the next six months, the panic episodes ceased never to recur again. But I knew it was time for professional help.

THERAPY

Although I had promised myself that I would seek out a therapist after the anxiety attacks, I put the idea on the back burner, not ready to deal with the causes quite yet. But within a few weeks, I was haunted by a different kind of demon: the Holocaust. Adam, now a toddler of ten or eleven months, got up in the middle of the night and stood in his crib, crying to be picked up. For a few nights, I did what any first-time mother would do. I took him out and rocked him until he fell back to sleep. I did this night after night, until I was so exhausted that I consulted our pediatrician. The pediatrician suggested that I allow Adam to cry for a few minutes to break the cycle. The doctor told me that after a few days, Adam would get used to putting himself back to sleep. I couldn't stand the crying. It wasn't normal crying.

As he cried, I stood and thought about all the babies and small children who had cried in hiding and in concentration camps. By not watching documentaries, reading Holocaust books, or hearing detailed accounts from my parents, I naively believed that small children also survived the camps. How does a mother explain to a baby that he or she shouldn't cry or make noise, or else he or she could be killed? How does a mother accept that she must allow her small child to starve to death? What happened to those small children who could not be stifled? I was haunted by these thoughts. I wanted to know the answers, but I couldn't bear to hear the facts. One day, my mother-in-law, not realizing my sensitivity, told me about what the Nazis had done to the babies.

"The Nazis took the babies and threw them against the brick wall, shattering their skulls," she blurted.

I asked my mother-in-law to stop because I couldn't bear to hear it. But it was too late. She had revealed enough of the haunting imagery that I would now work desperately to suppress.

My heart ached as I thought about those small victims. The only way I could stop the thoughts was to not let my son cry. I rocked him to sleep each night until eventually he stayed asleep for the night.

This marked the beginning of my on and off years in psychotherapy, or what I call "mute therapy." Most of my therapists didn't talk much. Between them not speaking and me being accustomed to the silent treatment, there wasn't much conversation. One of my therapists not only hardly spoke, she also fell asleep during our sessions. I called her the "boa lady" because she wore feathery neck scarves. My first therapist recommended the boa lady when I felt that she and I were at a therapeutic standstill. Not wanting to hurt her feelings, I told her I needed to find someone who was experienced with Holocaust survivors and their families. She gave me the name of the "boa lady," who was herself a survivor of the Holocaust and well known in the survivor community.

My relationship with the boa lady seemed off to a good start. Like when first meeting Gary or other children of Holocaust survivors or survivors themselves, there was an inherent bond. I tried hard to connect with her, to get to the point where I looked forward to our sessions. Within a few months, on a couple of occasions, I found myself standing outside her office for almost fifteen minutes before realizing she was not there. I telephoned her and left messages. She called me later to apologize, saying she had forgotten our weekly appointment.

Weeks later, I began to note the unimaginable: she was falling asleep during our sessions. After the first incident, I wasn't sure. But after several recurrences, there was no doubt in my mind. I knew I needed to leave or at least confront her.

I sat obediently, with self-discipline, as I watched her struggle to keep her eyes open and then give in to sleep for a few seconds. When she woke up, there were no apologies or any recognition of what had just happened. Week after week, I endured this unprofessional behavior, feeling responsible, thinking that if I were more interesting, talked more, or simply spoke with more inflection, I could prevent it. Each week, I promised myself that I would speak up, and each week her behavior reccurred. I sat and said nothing until one week when I had simply had enough.

I saw her eyelids become heavy, and she began to doze. A few minutes later, she woke up, startled. I sat quietly, and she repeated her usual line.

"What are you thinking about?"

That was my cue. I mustered up all my courage: "I am thinking about how you keep falling asleep on me."

I waited for the apology.

Instead, she looked at me and asked, "Have you ever felt this way with anyone else before?"

Her question implied that I had imagined her falling asleep. I never saw her again. I took a long therapeutic break.

A few years of calm followed with the birth of my second son, David. Four and a half years later, my third son, Jonathan, was born while I was in graduate school.

One day, in the course of my graduate studies, I was assigned a genealogy project. I filled in the facts I knew and then asked my mother and father to fill in what I did not know. To my surprise, my father gave me the names of two brothers: Stephan and Janus. I was shocked. Until then, he had led me to believe that he had only one brother, Stephan, who perished in the Holocaust.

My father matter-of-factly told me about his youngest brother, Janus, as though it was nothing new.

"Janus was seventeen in 1944 when the Nazis came to Hungary. He was born in 1927, when I was not at home because that was the year my parents sent me away to study at cheyder. I didn't see him much for the first two years. What I remember most about him as a baby is that when I went home to see him for the first time, he was in the baby carriage, and my father got agitated with him and hit him pretty badly for no good reason. He was just a baby and should never have been hit like that. Janus survived the war and went to Canada," he said.

I learned from my father that Janus went to Italy after the war, hoping to go to the United States or Canada; the only way to immigrate to Canada was to take a job in the coal mines. With no other choice, Janus seized the opportunity. My father explained that Janus became involved with a rough group of young men when he was twenty years old.

"One day, there was a terrible accident in the mine, and my brother was killed," my father said.

With other graduate courses and three children to take care of, this newly acquired piece of family history had to be put away and examined at a later time. Luckily, the postpartum depression and panic attacks that had followed Adam's birth did not recur. In fact, those were the calmest years I experienced with my parents. Those years were even enjoyable at times, especially with the kids.

One day, I saw an article in *The New York Times* about children of Holocaust survivors, which mentioned the names of two therapists. I called the first therapist, but she was not available. I tried the second therapist. She answered the phone and was willing to take me on as a client. Her name was Ruth Heber, and she herself was a child survivor of the Holocaust. I worked with her for several years. By that time, I realized my trauma stemmed more from my father's dysfunction than from the fact that my parents were Holocaust survivors. But this therapist and I established a solid and useful relationship. Not long after I started seeing her, I realized that my thoughts and visions of the Holocaust had diminished.

I soon began to have the first of a series of recurring dreams. In the dream, my husband and I wanted to buy a house. We found a house on a somewhat busy street in the middle of what appeared to be a town. It was a tall house, two to three stories, with wood on the outside. The house was not in a neighborhood I knew. We moved in. The house was an old, dilapidated, and abandoned mansion that was much bigger on the inside than it appeared on the outside. Downstairs was a movie theater with dusty, red velvet curtains and chairs. We went upstairs and stumbled over more bedrooms and then more levels and wings with added bedrooms. There was dust and cobwebs everywhere and holes in the aged floor.

As I stood in one of the upstairs bedrooms, rats came

up through the holes in the floor. Every room had holes, and every room had rats. Gary and I swung at them with whatever weapons we had, but they were endless. I found the bedroom with the fewest rats and battled them as they crept through the floor. I was determined to repair the house, clean it up, and get rid of the rats.

The first time I returned to the house in the dream, one of the upstairs bedrooms had been decorated in Laura Ashley pink. The floor was repaired, and the rats were gone, at least in that room of the house. The rest of the house remained the same rat-infested, haunted structure. The next time I visited, the theater had new red velvet curtains and seats. (The living room furniture in my childhood house had been red velvet as well.) On another occasion, the dream house was in a different location. The front faced a suburban street, and the back was steps away from the ocean's edge. The waves sometimes came so close that water would seep into the house. This dream recurred and changed many times over the next few years.

MY MOTHER MOVES IN

Once again, I was faced with losing my mother, but it was worse this time. As my mother complained to me of her weight loss, anorexia, and abdominal pain, my father interjected his proof that nothing was wrong with her. He could "prove" it with his meticulously kept, black marble composition book of *her* medical symptoms. He had a record that she had experienced the very same symptoms before, which turned out to be nothing more than stomach acid. With this "proof," he not only dismissed her symptoms, but also denied that she needed medical attention. I had to take matters into my own hands. I couldn't leave my mother in the hands of an irrational, delusional man. Something was wrong, and she needed urgent medical intervention.

An abdominal ultrasound revealed a pancreatic tumor, but whether it was malignant or benign would have to be determined. I made the arrangements, met with the surgeon, and discussed the options as my father turned a blind eye and a deaf ear. He showed his usual attitude: "I am not going to get involved. It is all yours. Do what you want with it." My mother was scheduled for a biopsy with the potential for surgery, depending on what they found and whether or not it was operable.

The night before her surgery, I stayed in my mother's hospital room with her until the end of visiting hours. We talked for hours. Never did my mother show fear. She had always accepted her fate. The Holocaust, and all the losses that went along with it, made her grateful for every minute that had been granted to her. I don't know what she did in private, but in front of me, she was strong. The day before her operation, I searched the Internet for information. Pancreatic cancer has an average survival time of six months, and fifty percent of people afflicted do not survive surgery. There was a significant chance, at age seventy-seven, that my mother would not survive surgery. I might not see her again. I went to the nurses' station for a piece of paper. They gave me two blank progress notes, which are what doctors and nurses use to write notes about hospitalized patients. I asked questions, and my mother talked. I used every bit of space on those two pages to write the facts about my mother and her Holocaust experience. That was one of the few times we discussed the Holocaust. I felt desperate.

Her operation took hours, and once again, my sister and I waited by ourselves in the same lonesome, second-floor waiting area at Mount Sinai where we had waited seventeen years earlier during our mother's breast cancer surgery. With every minute beyond the projected four hours for the surgery, we knew we faced a new malignancy.

The surgeon walked toward us and said, "Your mother has pancreatic cancer. The prognosis with surgery, radiation therapy, and chemotherapy is six to twelve months. Some are really lucky to survive three years."

My sister and I were devastated. I didn't know how I would tell my mother when she woke up, so I never did. Neither did the surgeon or the doctors.

I'm not surprised at my decision because in our home the word *cancer* was forbidden. It was equivalent to *mafia*, the word said softly so that no one would hear because mafia members had supersonic hearing that penetrated the walls of Brooklyn. If they heard you, your family could have "mafia trouble." If God hears you say *cancer*, He could strike you with it. Intuitively, however, my mother knew. It was very difficult to hide the "you have cancer" expression and the grief that goes along with it. She could read it on our faces. It was familiar.

My mother looked up compassionately at me from her bed in the recovery room, with a respirator and tubes. Her expression said, *I know, and it's OK. I'm sorry for you, and I appreciate all you do for me. It will be all right.* The doctors, nurses, my sister, and I did what medically needed to be done, but we never mentioned cancer or the prognosis.

She spent the next eight days in the ICU with a difficult postoperative recovery. My father never came to wish her well or comfort her. Throughout her entire hospital stay, whenever I visited, I found her sitting on the edge of her bed, leaning over so that she could peer at the door to see if someone was coming her way. I knew that she was waiting for me, but hoping for someone else.

His callousness and indifference was hard to digest. In addition, he was calculating and manipulative. He played a game to convince others that he was in poor health and was justified in not being respectful or attentive to my mother. He was a narcissistic liar.

As I sat at my mother's bedside waiting for respite, my father called the nurses' station to justify his failure to visit. The nurses and doctors came into my mother's room and announced that my father couldn't visit because his "blood pressure was very high." He needed to rest and was in danger of having a stroke.

It was hard for me to accept, as with my mother's breast cancer surgery and Levi's final days that my father was not going to acknowledge this crisis. I felt a tremendous burden being the only visitor at my mother's bedside day after day. My sister lived in Pennsylvania and came to visit on weekends, and my brother lived in California. I knew my mother waited for her husband, believing that this time, maybe this time, he would be different. My heart ached for her the way it had ached for

Levi years before. I wished that I could tell the bastard to get his g-ddamn ass to the hospital to see his dying wife, but I knew him better.

He finally arrived the morning she was being discharged, minutes before she was leaving to come home to my house to recuperate.

I took care of my mother until she was strong enough to stand again. The burden was not in caring for her, but in tending to my father's relentless demands for attention. He didn't want to be with her, and he didn't want to be without her—or, more likely, alone. He could not understand why all the attention had to be for my mother. "I'm alone. Anything can happen to me. I'm sick," he would tell me.

There were constant phone calls from him. He never stopped and barely asked how my mother was doing. She faced six weeks of radiation, five days a week and then indefinite chemotherapy, all of which was my responsibility. She stayed with me until she had finished the radiation and was ready to start the chemotherapy.

My mother had tremendous strength, remaining lighthearted throughout her illness. She never uttered a negative word or displayed self-pity. She accepted and lived every day with contentment.

The chemo was three weeks on and one week off in rotation. Each week, I drove to Brooklyn to pick her up, and then she stayed with me for a few days to make sure she was feeling well enough to return home to Brooklyn.

I noticed that each time I picked her up, her suitcase got bigger—much bigger than it should have been for a two-day stay. My friend Randi stated the obvious one day: "Face it. She wants to move in."

These words surprised me, though they shouldn't have. My father made her stay in Brooklyn more and more unpleasant. When my mother first returned to Brooklyn, which she loved, he had moved the furniture around in a way that said, *This house is mine, you don't live here anymore, and you are not welcome.* He moved his army cot into the living room, where he now slept. A shower curtain now hung between the living room and dining room, and the entire dining room table was now filled from one end to the other with his "stuff" neatly lined up. Rubber bands, pens and pencils, writing pads, and eating utensils were everywhere. The entire house now took on the same psychotic order as his bedroom, and it was hard to witness. He had moved into the living room, and he was not moving out. It was an extension of "his territory." My mother had been stripped of her identity within her own home. It no longer belonged to her.

One day, when I picked up my mother from her short stay in Brooklyn, she reported that day after day my father walked past her as she lay on the couch and did not say a word to her. Occasionally, she asked my father to pick up something for her at the grocery store, and his response was simply "no," or he walked past her and pretended not to hear her request. I hated him for not helping her, and I hated him for not recognizing that I was caring for three small children and needed respite from taking care of my mother.

The irony was that my mother's terminal illness liberated her and gave us the gift of being together without the static and control of my father. The illness gave us three wonderful years together, and living in my home gave my mother the sustenance she so deserved.

She was a gift to me and my family. Despite the illness and the ongoing chemotherapy treatments, she brought a wonderful joy into our home, the kind of joy only a loving grandmother can give. She was Jonathan's built-in nanny, and they were blessed with innocence between grandchild and grandparent. My mother adored him as she did all children. She cared for the house and was my friend. She was available and willing to help whenever we needed her. The warmth and acceptance of our household infused her with a kind of peace that I had never seen in her before.

For the first time in many years, she was surrounded by calm. There was no fighting, no anger, no silent treatment, no disrespect, no sadistic manipulation. We loved and respected her, and she us. We soon noticed that the "essential tremor" she had had for so many years began to disappear. My mother was the first to note it as she proudly announced, "I no longer need Librium. Did you notice that my head doesn't shake much anymore?"

I hadn't noticed until she mentioned it, but it was true. The rhythmic shaking of her head that sometimes lasted for hours was gone.

In our home, despite my father's callousness, she still waited for his phone calls. He didn't call; he waited for me to call him. He then calculated the number of days before he could call and berate me by demanding required intervals between my phone calls. I tried to conform to his scheduling demands. Still imprinted in my neurons was that with him, "no" was not an option. I never argued and hardly questioned. He was irrational, and so I telephoned him under duress.

Not once did I call him willingly or with any warmth. I dreaded the sound of his voice. My actions were robotic. I felt obliged to fulfill the moral parameters I had set for myself as a daughter, and I obediently did as was expected. Occasionally, I did not conform. Instead, I stretched the "specifications," desiring one more day of respite before I heard his voice. His voice took me into despair. The conversation was a chore, strained in every imaginable way. It unfailingly revolved around the word *I.* Sometimes, for my own amusement, I tried to count how many times he said the word *I* in our conversation.

The phone calls with my father, whether made out of guilt or his tyranny, never mentioned my mother. Not a single word. She was dying, yet he would not ask about her. My conversations with him were not only dreaded because of his anger, guilt, and self-centeredness, but also because my mother knew he was on the telephone and sat waiting next to me in anticipation of her turn to speak to him. She listened to the conversation, waiting for the cue that he had asked about her or wanted to speak with her, which never happened.

One day, against my usual, expected routine, I defied him. After I had had enough of our conversation, I handed my mother the phone and said, "Here, he wants to speak to you," which of course he did not. He spoke with her, which I could tell by her expression made her happy. The next time he called, before he even said hello, he said, "The last time I called, you gave the phone to your mother. Please do not give her the phone again." Sometimes I did, and sometimes I didn't. He was going to have to live with that if he wanted to call my house.

Over the next three years, my mother seldom went home to Brooklyn, and my father never came to see her; therefore, they saw each other very little. The only contact they had was on holidays or birthdays when they were both invited by the extended family. My father was just fine with that arrangement.

On the few occasions that we visited Brooklyn, I was reluctantly told by neighbors about the "woman with the red car" who frequented my mother's home. Now I knew why my father made sure that my mother did not feel comfortable in her own home. He didn't want her there. I wasn't surprised by him, but I hoped that my mother wouldn't find out. I never told her.

THE LOSS OF MY MOTHER

For a while, my mother was able to tolerate the weekly chemotherapy, and her condition was stable. I was so grateful that she was alive and not suffering from her illness, despite having received such a poor prognosis. At times, I walked past her bedroom in our home, and when I was certain she was asleep, I entered the room and quietly walked to her bed. I then stretched my arms over her body as I placed my hands in the air, inches over her abdomen. In nursing school, I had taken a class on "therapeutic touch," and although I had no idea what I was doing, I thought it was worth a try and figured it could certainly do no harm. I concentrated as I imagined areas in need of healing. I don't know if it was "therapeutic touch" or "magical thinking," but for a while she beat the odds for survival. Even the oncologists were surprised that the metastatic tumors inside her liver had not progressed.

But despite the therapeutic touch, love, and happiness, she began to lose ground and succumb to her illness after three and a half years. As her condition worsened, I felt compelled to tell my father, as I did everyone else in the family, that she was not doing well. The doctors determined that she probably would not survive more than a few months. Whatever the situation was between my parents, my father was still her husband, and I felt he had the right to know that she was dying. Maybe if he knew it was really the end, he could muster enough compassion to touch her heart, even if it meant faking it.

To my surprise and disgust, about two months after telling my father of my mother's prognosis, he said without reservation or emotion, "I thought you told me that your mother would not survive more than a few more months." It seems he had taken "a few more months" to mean literally "two." His implication was that I had disappointed and cheated him.

On November 9, 2000, my beloved mother died in her own bedroom at my house. The Jewish date was Heshvan 11, which coincided with the *Yahrzeit* (death anniversary) of Rachel, the matriarch of the Jewish people. During her last moments, she was surrounded by the love and attention of my family. She had been deteriorating over the last month, but she made every effort to take care of her own needs. It broke my heart as I watched her struggle for breath those last few days.

The hospice nurse arrived the week before my mother died and informed me that one of the requirements for hospice was that I accept my mother's fate and not intervene medically. I was not to take her to the hospital or emergency room if she were to deteriorate. I reluctantly agreed. To this day, I still struggle with the question of what more I should have done. The nurse told me that my mother needed to be comfortable and that they would manage her pain so that she could end her life without suffering. She placed a fentanyl patch on my mother's chest to relieve her pain and gave me a bottle of liquid morphine to use at my discretion. My mother didn't complain of much pain, but when she did, I gave her the morphine and hoped that between it and the fentanyl patch, she would not suffer.

Looking at my mother asleep, more comfortable than she had been in weeks, I decided to run out and do some errands for an hour or so. When I came back, her respirations had become so shallow that I knew I was losing her. She wasn't asleep; she was dying. I called her name and gently shook her, but there was no response. I couldn't rouse her, and I wasn't ready to let her go.

As a nurse, I knew that the shallow respirations were most likely the result of narcotics, so I ripped the fentanyl patch from her chest, and within a half hour, she began to wake up. I was so relieved but not quite sure that I had done the right thing. She was so peaceful and had perhaps even accepted her destiny, but I was not ready to lose her, not yet. I couldn't bear the idea of never seeing her again.

The last week of my mother's life was so unbearable that I felt I had no choice but to let it end. She was suffering, and there was nothing more to do but let her go. She slept during the day and was awake all night. We hired a nurse's aide to stay with her at night so that I could get some sleep, but it didn't work. The nurse's aide was not very motivated and seemed bothered that my mother couldn't sleep. The aide wanted to sleep, and my mother was not cooperating. It didn't matter because my mother relentlessly hollered my name. "Keti, Keti, Keti," she yelled repeatedly. As I came to her bedside at 3:00 a.m., I didn't know what to say or do for her. She kept calling my name, and I desperately wanted to comfort her.

The night before she died, she repeated something in Hungarian when I came into the room. Not understanding Hungarian, I wasn't sure what she was saying, but her pleading tone made me believe that she was asking God to have mercy on her and let her die. At that moment, I decided to let her die.

The next day, my children had a day off from school. My mother said that she was thirsty, and I gave her a few teaspoons of melted, cherry-flavored ice. When the hospice nurse arrived at about 10:00 a.m., she pulled the comforter off my mother and looked down at my mother's feet. They had turned blue overnight.

She led me out of the room and said, "Your mother is dying."

"Do you think it will be days or hours?" I asked, explaining that I needed to notify my sister.

"Hours," the hospice nurse answered.

I called my sister and reached her husband, who asked me if we thought it could wait until Liz finished work at three o'clock. I turned and asked the nurse.

"She should come right now," the nurse said.

My sister left Bryn Mawr, Pennsylvania, for a two-and-a-half-hour drive as soon as she got the news.

Fortunately, my three sons were across the street, playing at my neighbor's house. I pulled a chair close to my mother's bed and sat, holding her hand, trying to give her a few more teaspoons of the cherry ice, which slowly dripped down her chin. She mumbled something in Hungarian about her sister Boreshka, the one who was taken on the SS wagon during the death march and never seen again. I could not understand it, but in an odd, eerie way, I felt Boreshka's presence. My mother turned and looked at me. Her eyes opened wide as she took two quick breaths, and she was gone.

My sister had not yet arrived, so I pleaded with my mother to wait. "Ima, Ima, Sheva is coming! Please wait!" I cried out. It was no use. My mother lay motionless.

I telephoned my neighbor Laurie to tell her that my mother had just died. She immediately came over. She knew my mother and was not afraid to see her dead, so she came into the room with me. The boys sensed that something had happened, and they soon came running home. I told them that Ima had died, but that we had done such a great job loving her and taking care of her that we had provided her with a miracle. The doctors had said she would only live six months, but with us helping her, she had lived an amazing three and a half years. I asked the boys if they wanted to go into the room to say goodbye to her.

My baby, Jonathan, barely five years old at the time, went first. He pulled himself up onto her bed and sat nestled between my mother and the wall, looking at her and touching her in a beautiful way, symbolic of the relationship that they had shared for most of his life. He sat and looked at her, but he instinctively understood that she had to go. My middle son, David, was next. He was the one who always went out of his way to do a little something extra for her, even when it meant not being a "real boy" at nine years old, such as holding her pocketbook when she walked to lighten her load. Adam, my oldest son, who was twelve, opted for his own personal reasons not to go in, but his loss was no less great. I wanted the boys to have closure in whatever way they chose.

A few minutes later, the hospice nurse returned. Her first words to me were "She is only a shell now. Her spirit is gone." With those words, for the first time, I could let her go. I knew that she would live on with us and that I would never lose her. Her spirit, her lessons, her touch, her warmth, her kindness would be infused in all whom she had touched.

A few minutes after that, my sister walked into the house to the news that our mother had died. I am grateful that the hospice nurse was there to intercept my sister and relieve me of the burden of telling her that she had not arrived in time to say goodbye to our mother. As I sat upstairs on the bed with my lifeless mother, I heard my sister's terrible, screeching wail coming from downstairs.

Shortly thereafter, Gary arrived home and called the funeral home. After two to three hours, two suited men arrived to take my mother's body away. We were to drive to the funeral home to discuss the funeral preperations.

At the funeral home, the funeral director asked, "Do you want the Jewish shroud outfit with the veil? And how about the yeshiva boy who watches over the body and prays until you are ready for the burial?"

These were questions I had never discussed with my mother. Who could I ask now? I compromised and opted for half of the Jewish shroud outfit and half of the outfit that I thought looked best on her. The coffin was cushy despite the traditional Jewish pine box that was her family's tradition, and she would be kept warm with the blanket that she had used the last few years. I found it difficult, even after she was dead, to stop taking care of her.

A bigger challenge was finding a rabbi because neither my mother nor father was affiliated with any synagogue. Although she had grown up as an Orthodox Jew, by my father's doing she was not affiltiated to any rabbi. I didn't like the Orthodox "dial-a-rabbi" from Boro Park that my cousin had used for my aunt the year before, and I didn't feel particularly close to my rabbi or believe that he was an option. I asked the funeral director to recommend a rabbi and tested my luck even further.

"If possible, could you find someone who is connected to the Holocaust?" I asked.

To my surprise, the funeral director mentioned Rabbi Unger from the congregation in Woodcliff Lakes, New Jersey. He described him as a Hungarian Holocaust survivor.

The funeral director said, "I highly doubt that he will do it. He is retired and is very selective about what he is willing to do these days, but because your mother was also a Hungarian Holocaust survivor, I will ask."

That evening, the funeral director called me and, to my great relief, said that Rabbi Unger had agreed to do the funeral service.

I got to work on both the eulogy and the rabbi's speech, assuming that he wouldn't have much to say because he didn't know my mother. I wanted everything to be perfect. I wanted my mother to be honored on her departure. My brother came from California, and my father, whom I expected to put up a fuss, arrived without a word.

We gathered at the funeral home, and the director asked us who would like to go in to view my mother's body before they closed the casket. Without hesitation, I volunteered to go in. She was my mother, my child, my friend. I was her caregiver, and I was going to see to it that she was put to rest in a way that I deemed acceptable. As I looked at her, I knew that we would both be at peace.

My mother lay in her cushy, fluffed blue satin coffin with the *yeshiva bocher* beside her. She wore a veil, like a bride, and she looked beautiful and restful. I bent over and kissed her on the forehead. I opened her crossed arms just enough so that I could place the framed picture of Boreshka beneath her hands, close to her heart. I said, without speaking, *Go to Boreshka. She is waiting for you.* I was at peace because with my mother's burial, Boreshka was also being put to rest.

I went out to the family meeting room at the funeral home where the rest of my family was waiting. The rabbi came out and said he wanted to see my sister, my brother, my father, and me privately for a few minutes in his quarters. We dutifully followed him. My father sat without saying a word. He asked a few questions. I handed the rabbi his speech. He looked at me perplexed because he had asked me to jot down a few things about my mother; instead, I had written an entire speech. We all got up to go back outside to greet our guests except for my sister, who turned to the rabbi and said, "May I speak with you privately for a few minutes?" What they spoke about I don't know.

While they were out of the room, my father turned to me and disclosed the following:

"I know this rabbi. I know his whole family from Hungary. As a matter of fact, his grandfather was the rabbi in the same synagogue in Nagyteteni where my father was the cantor. His grandfather had four sons and, I think, four daughters. One son became a dentist, one became a doctor, and two became lawyers. His father was one of the sons who became a lawyer. When I left the military hospital, I returned to my forced labor unit in the Hungarian army. I wanted to desert the army. I heard that his uncle, the dentist, whom I had known because he was our local dentist, was working in the Swedish embassy in Budapest where they had given out some 3,000 'Schutz passes.' One of the men from our unit was making a run to the embassy for those passes. I sent a note with him to give to Dr. Unger. He returned with thirty Schutz passes and called out names. The last one was mine. That document gave me the confidence to desert. His father, the lawyer, is another story. As I've told you, at that time, the Jews of Hungary were declared 'stateless.' His father promised to help us obtain Hungarian citizenship. He filled out and sent in all the documents, but he forgot to put his stamp on them, so we never received citizenship."

Now I knew why he had sat so quietly in the rabbi's quarters. I wasn't sure how to react to the story or whether it was the right time for my father to be sharing it.

The funeral was a farewell tribute to a woman loved by everyone. I could feel the warmth and love that surrounded her. She would always be remembered as a compassionate, kind, and caring person. She would truly be missed. From the funeral, we drove silently in our limousines to the cemetery. I waited in the calm before the storm. It was unlikely that there would be an extended visit among my sister, brother, and father without an eruption. It was inevitable. I hoped that out of respect for my mother, they might stay in control.

The coffin was placed in the ground. We took turns placing shovelfuls of dirt on top of the coffin in the way that many Jewish people say goodbye to a loved one at a burial. My father stood alone. For a moment, his despair was convincing, but I knew too much. As far as I was concerned, he didn't deserve the privilege of being there. But for reasons I will never understand, he meant something to my mother. She deserved his respect as she was being laid to rest. Next to my mother's grave, at my father's request, was the abutting grave I had purchased for him. From the cemetery, we went back to my house to start the traditional seven days of shiva (the Jewish period of official mourning).

I not only had to think of my brother, sister, and father getting along during shiva, but I was again having one of my all-too-common childhood flashbacks. I was about to break Rule 2; my mother's family from Boro Park, who were forbidden from entering our house by my father, were arriving. This time, it was my house. I, at age forty-one, still feared that they were forbidden. I waited for them to arrive and for my father's inevitable agitation. I knew that he was capable of an outbreak at any time. He had proven it over and over again: the interrogations, the eavesdropping, the phone rage, and the neighbor's kids. His attacks and irrational outbursts had no limits. I hoped that my mother's death and the respect she deserved would deter him.

Soon after we arrived home, my father asked my brother, whom he had not spoken to in years, to help him search for a site on the Internet. Shortly after, my brother came out of the computer room with a look of disgust and disbelief on his face.

"Can you believe he asked me to show him how to find a lady partner on the Internet?" my brother announced.

My sister marched to where my father was still sitting at the computer and screamed at him, "How can you ask your son, who just buried his mother, to help you find a woman? You are a little man!"

She stormed out of the room. My brother announced that he was leaving, and my sister followed a day later, leaving me with my father. After my sister and brother had gone, I waited for the next confrontation. I wondered what my mother would think if she knew that even at her shiva her husband and children could not behave. She wouldn't have been surprised. It was predictable, but it was also shocking and sad.

On the third evening, the "forbidden" Boro Park entourage arrived with the head matriarch, my mother's first cousin, Aranka Moskowitz. We'd lived in her building in Boro Park when we first came to America. With her, came her sons, George and Moishe, and their wives, Michelle and Olga. They marched in, each one of them carrying trays full of Aranka's homemade Jewish specialties, enough to feed twenty people for a week. I was deeply touched and knew that my mother would have been as well. We stood and talked in the living room as my father sat in the kitchen, refusing to come in to greet them.

With my father, I was never too sure if it was that he hated them or was afraid that they, for good reason, hated him. As my cousin George left the living room to go to the kitchen, I had the familiar feeling of intense fear. I held my breath as I pretended to listen to the conversation around me, but what I was really listening for was the outbreak in the kitchen. Within a few minutes, George returned to the living room.

He put his arm on my father's shoulder and said, "Look who I found? It's Laci. He looks great. I haven't seen him in so many years."

I mused, *If he had his choice, you wouldn't have seen him for so many more years.* Then I thought to myself, *Bless you, George. Bless you for being so morally mature to fake this for me.*

MY FATHER MOVES IN

My mother's death was followed by a few months of calm. Within two months of her death, I began working on a project at our town school in Demarest, New Jersey. It was a very special annual event called International Day. In March each year, our entire lower grade school was transformed into various countries for the children and parents to enjoy. There would be food, arts and crafts, skits, and dances from the countries the PTA had chosen for that year. This year, the chosen countries were Israel and Armenia, and I was given the honor of chairing the Israel committee. In my mind, it was a tribute to my mother. Working on that event so shortly after my mother's death helped ease the day-to-day pain of losing her.

The school year was ending, Adam and David were scheduled for sleep away camp in July, and Jonathan would go to day camp. I anticipated a summer of rest.

A day or two after Adam and David left for sleepaway camp, I got a phone call. A man introducing himself as a Brooklyn firefighter announced that he was with my father in the basement of my father's house in Brooklyn.

"Your father fell in the basement, and he seems to have hurt his leg."

I asked the man how he fell.

The firefighter responded, "I've asked him, but he says he doesn't know. He doesn't know what happened, except that he fell and hurt his leg. He doesn't know how it happened."

I thought, *Yeah, right. He didn't fall. It's just another one of his tactical maneuvers to try to get me to take him in.* He must have intentionally done something to himself so that I would finally take him into my home, which he had been hinting at since my mother passed away.

The firefighter went on to say that my father refused to let them take him to the hospital. My father told the firefighters that I would come and take him. *Of course,* I thought. *I can't think of anything better I would like to do with my break than spend time with my father.*

"He's asking us to make him some tea," the firefighter continued. "We're very busy. We can't stay here and make him a tea."

I couldn't help but laugh as I thought, *Yep, that sure sounds like my father.* It would never cross his mind that Brooklyn firefighters might have a serious job to do. Laci wanted tea, and they should serve him. I assured the firefighter that I would be there shortly. They left without making him the tea.

I soon arrived to take my father to Mount Sinai Hospital. As soon as we entered the emergency room, I could see that he was euphoric.

"*Señorita, muy bonita,*" he said, flirting with the Hispanic women. He was elated because he had center stage. He was at the hospital, with me, getting attention. He also sensed that he was soon to be in my home. He had obtained his ticket in. I sat with him, waiting for the X-ray results as he flirted with anyone and everyone, and I thought, *Please, God, don't let anything be broken. Please let him go back home.*

The emergency room doctor walked in and said, "Good news. Nothing is broken. Must just be a bad sprain."

"How long until he is well enough to walk?" I asked.

"Four or five days. A week at most," he answered.

OK, I thought, *a week out of my free month with the kids at camp. I can handle that.* It could have been worse. It could have been broken, and he could have had to stay with me much longer. They put a brace on his leg and told us to follow up with his orthopedist.

I broke the news to my husband. My father was coming to stay for a few days. We moved a folding sleeper chair downstairs to the dining room so that my father wouldn't have to climb the steps. Within a few feet were the bathroom and the kitchen, so he wouldn't have to walk far. Unfortunately, this spot was also the center of our house. Each time I moved anywhere, he noticed and called out, "Keti, bring me this. Keti, bring me that." There was no escape. Four days passed, then five, and to my despair, his leg had not improved much. I was growing more and more impatient with his demands, and I resented having him in my home. I wanted him out and quickly. I was exhausted and needed a break both mentally and physically. I had so looked forward to my much-needed calm.

One day, as my father hobbled around my kitchen, which he had taken over with his system of tea bags, pots and pans, and whatever else he wanted in special places, he turned to me and said, "Ima told me when she was living in your house that she really wanted to live with me in Brooklyn and not in your house because she didn't really feel welcomed here."

I knew it wasn't true, but even if it was, how dare he say it to me now. To me, who for three and a half years had taken my mother for chemo, radiation, and second opinions. To me, who had fed her, comforted her, loved her, and sat beside her as she took her last breath while he was off with the "woman with the red car." How dare he slap me in the face like that? He never ceased to amaze me.

One day, because he was agitated at me for not giving in to his every whim and whimper, he decided he had nothing left to hurt my mother with now that she was gone, so he said, "You know that grave next to your mother? I don't want it. I don't want to be buried near her."

I thought, *You damn bastard, you should never be privileged enough to lie next to her.*

MY FATHER MOVES OUT

Itook my father to the orthopedist, who agreed that he should have had more improvement by now. "He needs an MRI, which might be able to pick up something that was not picked up on the earlier X-ray in the emergency room," the orthopedist said. *Oh please no,* I thought. *Not something more.*

We went for the MRI, and it was confirmed: a broken patella. He had a broken kneecap, and surgery was the only way to fix it. He would have to stay in the hospital two to three days and then convalesce for two or three weeks before he was ready to start weeks of physical therapy. I felt doomed, overcome by the thought of not being able to rid myself of his unbearable presence. My summer break passed before my eyes. I had had enough and didn't know how I could handle him for much longer, but I didn't see any alternative. He would not consent to anyone else helping him. Even if he did, he was so obnoxious that it would not be easy to keep anyone around for long. I did the only thing I felt I could do. I called my therapist and asked her for the name of a psychiatrist. I went to see the psychiatrist, and I requested that she medicate me because I was at my wit's end. Paxil it would be for the next six months.

Gary and I went to the hospital early on the evening of his surgery, but my father was not yet out of the recovery room. We had plans for a party, and I felt no obligation to be there with him. I had made as much of an effort as I was willing to make. He was still in the recovery room, so we left for the party. Making these assertive moves was always easier with my husband at my side. Shortly after we arrived at the party, my cell phone rang. It was my father's nurse telling me that he had arrived in his room and that he was cursing and screaming at all the nurses, even referring to one as "the black bitch." He was upset that I hadn't been there when he woke up. I should have known that he would not make it easy. I could do as I wanted, but I was going to pay for it.

I turned to Gary and told him that I had no choice but to go back to the hospital. When I entered my father's hospital room, he lay in bed, refusing to acknowledge me and not saying a word. He didn't have to say anything because he wore the "Laci look." I took comfort in the fact that by returning, I had potentially tamed him for the night. I went to the nurses' station and asked to speak to them for a minute. They invited me into the nurses' lounge and shared stories of his outbursts.

"I'm sorry," I said. "Please don't take it personally." I told them of his family's demise during the Holocaust and how this had affected his life. I had resorted to this explanation in the past when I needed to justify his behaviors, especially when he had offended people. It potentially made those who dealt with him do so with a little more empathy. I apologized and asked them not to take his actions or words to heart.

After a few days, he was ready to be discharged from the hospital, back to my dining room. This time, it would not be for a few days. Post surgery, he became more demanding, and I became less tolerant. One day, after I had helped him with everything he needed and more, I told him I was going to go out for a while. He had washed, eaten his breakfast, drank his tea, gone to the bathroom, and been tucked into his fresh bed.

He looked up at me from his dining room bed and asked, "Where are you going?"

"Out," I said, feeling he deserved no more explanation than that.

He replied in a quivering voice, "Don't leave me."

"What do you mean, don't leave you?" I asked.

He was in bed and settled after his relentless demands of the morning. I was sure that although he preferred my help, he was perfectly capable of doing most things for himself. Although it wasn't comfortable for him, he could maneuver to get up and about if he needed to.

Again, but this time more forcefully, I said, "I'm going out."

From his bed, he pleaded, "Please, please don't leave me here alone. Have mercy on me. I'll die if you leave me here alone."

Not before I kill you, I thought.

Rage built up inside me.I turned to him and shouted, "You are a fucking pig! You don't give a damn about anyone but yourself!"

I don't remember what more I said, but it wasn't pretty. It was a fit of rage, long coming. It gave me tremendous satisfaction. I walked out and slammed the front door. From that day on, he was afraid that if he pushed me far enough, I could attack. I decided then that it was him or me. One of us had to leave, and I elected him. I told him that he had until the first of August to return to his home in Brooklyn.

"I'm never returning to Brooklyn," he said. "I don't want to go back to that house. I'm finished with it. I want to stay with you the way your mother did."

"Not happening," I told him.

If he didn't want to go back to Brooklyn, I would help him find an apartment in New Jersey, which had originally been his wish.

But after a while, I knew differently. We looked at apartments, or—should I say—I did because he showed no interest while we were there and always found something wrong. He had one ideal place in mind: my house. Because of his narcissism, he believed that if he planned it, it would work. Not this time.

Through a friend, I found him an apartment in Cresskill, New Jersey, which was near where I lived in Demarest. My mother-in-law provided the name of two housekeepers to be interviewed to care for him. This was the plan whether he liked it or not. My newly acquired friend Paxil was kicking in, giving me inner strength. I meant business.

The first woman came. She was from Haiti and a bit assertive, but my father was respectful of her during the interview.

As soon as she left, he said, "I don't like her."

"OK. Another housekeeper is coming," I said.

This woman was Hungarian. Her nephew worked with my mother-in-law's friend. Her name was Gizi. She was fifty-seven years old, quiet, modestly dressed, spoke a little English, and seemed reasonable. He entertained her with conversation and seemed to enjoy her.

As soon as she left, I asked, "So what do you think?"

"I don't like her either," he answered.

"Well, I do, and you have to make a choice between the Haitian and the Hungarian," I said. "If you can't choose, I'll make the choice for you. It will be the Hungarian woman."

The Hungarian it was. She would start in three days, and he would move into his apartment with her. It was August first, a few days after my boys had arrived home from camp. My entire summer break had passed me by.

With the plans for my father's departure from my home finalized, I would finally get some peace. He took a liking to Gizi, and by a miracle, she grew fond of him. The only problem was that he found it hard to define the relationship. He didn't quite understand that she worked for him and was not there as his girlfriend or for his pleasure. She helped him through his convalescence, and then they went dancing together and took frequent trips to Brooklyn. On one of his visits to the cardiologist, he privately asked for Viagra. She accepted his controlling behaviors without much fuss. On their trips to Brooklyn, he demanded that she wear a babushka on her head as she boarded the bus so that she could pass as a senior citizen and get the reduced rate. One day, he asked me for my mother's Medicaid card so that "Gizi could use it on the bus." The audacity of him to offer my dead mother's identity to someone else! It was a desecration.

"Like hell, she will," I said.

He still demanded my presence, and he manipulated Gizi to call me many times with "Your father is not well" so that I would come over and visit. Once, he insisted that he was weak and dizzy and urgently needed to be taken to the hospital. I knew from my nursing training and my knowledge of his character that there was nothing wrong with him. He decided that he needed a thorough evaluation, and he had determined that this was the most efficient way to get one. It was his usual, manipulative nonsense. We went to the emergency room at Mount Sinai Hospital. Of course, they found nothing wrong with him. I took the opportunity to ask for help. I went to the nurses' station and asked for a piece of paper on which I wrote the following: *Please call a psychiatrist. He is depressed.*

When the doctor came in to examine him, I held up the paper so that only the doctor could see it. He called a psychiatric resident, who came down to see my father and questioned him about depression.

"My dear wife," my father began, "may her soul rest in peace, died a year ago. It was a terrible shock for me."

You lying bastard, I thought. He knew all the right things to say. Of course, the psychiatrist believed him. Why not? It sounded normal. But my father was far from normal, and he didn't give a damn about my mother being sick. The psychiatrist gave him an appointment for the following week.

The next week, we went to see the psychiatrist. My father thanked him for his services and said that he preferred to see someone privately in New Jersey. I was thrilled that he would entertain the thought at all. I made an appointment with a local geriatric psychiatrist. My father snowed him, too, with the "terrible shock of losing my wife" story. He started taking the prescribed antidepressants, and he stopped taking them after two days.

Gizi had come to America with her twenty-six-year-old daughter, Kotika, and her son-in-law, Jolte, who was married to her other daughter, Anika, who remained behind in Hungary. They were a package deal. It didn't

make much sense to me, but as long as it worked, I
didn't care too much. Gizi was very attached to Kotika
and often took days off to see her. At first, Kotika spent a
night or two with Gizi in my father's apartment, and he
was hospitable, as he often was in the beginning. But he
soon put an end to that. Like everyone else in his life, he
soon despised the daughter altogether and forbade her
from coming to the apartment. Soon, Gizi had to meet
her daughter somewhere else.

Five years after Gizi began taking care of my father,
Kotika met and married an American who was in the
military. They announced that they would move in a few
months to Germany, where he would be stationed. Gizi
announced that she would leave with them to go back to
her family in Hungary. But before she left, Gizi offered
to help interview Hungarian women as her replacement.

Together, Gizi and my father interviewed over twenty
Hungarian women for the job, and they could not agree
on one. The time came for Gizi to leave, and in a frenzy,
we hired a woman at the last minute. We met her first,
and Gizi approved. She would start the next day and
overlap with Gizi's last four days so that she could be
trained. I picked her up in Manhattan, and she cried
the entire way, saying that Gizi had insulted her on the
phone by calling her a gypsy. I assured her that Gizi liked
her and that it was going to work out. Actually, I had my
doubts as I watched her emotional weakness.

Gizi, indeed, did not like her and was not shy about
letting her know. The woman also refused to leave her

bedroom door open. "No way, no how," she said even after Gizi explained that my father was old and scared and that this way she could hear if he needed something. Gizi convinced my father that the woman was a gypsy, and they both knew that gypsies from Hungary couldn't be trusted. Gizi said the woman had a gypsy maiden name, which the woman had concealed. Gizi confronted her about this as though it was a crime. Insulted, the woman left within two days. I drove the woman back to where I had picked her up, and she rambled in Hungarian the entire way, most of which I did not understand.

Then came the too-good-to-be-true intellectual. She was smart, pretty, middle aged, and spoke perfect English. My father watched every move she made and instructed her on every aspect of housekeeping as though she was an imbecile.

He used the same routine with all the women that he had used with my mother and us children when we lived at home. He believed only he knew how to do things right and that without his detailed instruction and surveillance, we would surely mess up. With these women, just as with us, there was a special routine for washing dishes and for preparing his food. There were rules about what cleaning solutions they were allowed to use, which were pretty much none, as well as how and when they could open the windows and for how long and for how many inches. The curtains were to always stay drawn, the oven was never to be used, and his clothes were to be washed by hand. A minimal amount of money was to be spent on food. As a matter of fact, he had food delivered weekly from Shomer Shabbos, a Jewish charity for the needy, and that food was to be their main diet. He constantly policed the caretakers, which made it impossible for any of them to exist with him. The intellectual woman stayed for about a week. She left me a note: *You are a kind person. Your father is an eccentric man. I am truly sorry for you.*

The next woman, a rather nice, blonde who was an acquaintance of the last caretaker and jealous that she had not gotten the job, thought she was on her way to vacationing at a health spa. She was very excited about inheriting the job. It looked easy to her. My father was good looking, bright, very friendly (at first), and did not require any physical care. It was mainly companionship, or so she thought. As we approached the neighborhood, I sensed her excitement as she mapped out her future walking route. Within a few days, she was singing a different tune. She did not have enough of the "special food" that she needed. My father demanded that she not go out as often as she did for her exercise, and at one point, he began locking her out. She ranted and raved in Hungarian. I looked to my father for translation as he happily said, "She wants to leave." *Duh!* I thought. That was it; I drove her back as well.

Next, we had the Hungarian dictator. I called her that because she came with rules. I thought my father had finally met his match. She demanded that he be in bed at 8:00 p.m. and that he not leave or get up from his bed or walk around until morning. Surprisingly, he obeyed her and obediently pissed in a milk container by his bed so that he would not get up to disturb the woman in the middle of the night. Instead, they fought over the heat. Too hot, too cold. Air conditioner on, air conditioner off. With the same window restrictions as the others, she said that she was suffocating and couldn't take it anymore. She quit.

And then came number six, the final contender. She was a cheerful, robust redhead Hungarian who did not speak a single word of English. I hired her without ever meeting her because she came as a friend of Jolte's, Gizi's son-in-law. She smiled a lot and seemed pleasant, but he was not fond of her from the minute she walked in. He blatantly refused to eat her food and simply said, "She can't cook." He ignored her, but she stayed and remained understanding and pleasant.

At that point, I contacted a social worker named Vicki, who worked as a care manager for the elderly and was extremely familiar with Holocaust survivors. She came in weekly to visit my father. It was clear that the loss of Gizi and the difficulty with six new caretakers was too much for him. He stopped eating and sleeping. Vicki recommended a psychiatrist/rabbi whom my father had willingly seen a few times. This psychiatrist gave my father the antidepressant mitrazapine, but my father was extremely paranoid about medication (that is, when someone other than himself prescribed the medications), so he took the antidepressants for a few days and then stopped. He was also being heavily medicated with an assortment of Hungarian bootleg medications that Gizi continued to supply him after she returned to Hungary, despite my repeated demands for her to stop. There were tranquilizers, antianxiety pills, analgesics, antipyretics, and sleep medications. He took Gizi's medications without reservation. He refused food, lost weight, no longer went out, and pretty much stayed in bed all day. He refused to interact with the smiling woman and claimed he never slept.

On November 9, 2005, the fifth-year anniversary of my mother's death, we had an appointment to see the psychiatrist. I picked up my father at his apartment. To my surprise, as we walked over to my car, he said, "I'm going to tell Dr. S. that I want to go into the hospital."

Baruch HaShem (Thank God), I thought. I didn't believe my ears. This wasn't the first time he had said those words. He had used them several times over the last few weeks, and I thought that he was saying it once again for dramatic effect. In my wildest dreams, I would never have believed that my father would consent to a stay in a psychiatric unit, let alone ask to be sent there. For me, this was a dream come true. But he didn't recognize that he was the one with the problem. He believed his depression was about the caretakers and

Gizi leaving him. It may have been that he believed this was his ticket back into my home, but I was not going to fall into that trap again. I had to think ahead of him at all times.

We got to the doctor's office. As usual, I stayed in the waiting area after the psychiatrist called my father in. His office was right across the street from Englewood Hospital.

The psychiatrist eventually came out and said to me, "Your father says that he wants to be hospitalized. I don't think it is a bad idea."

I said, "I know," trying hard to contain my excitement.

My father and I walked across the street as the doctor made the necessary phone calls to alert the doctors and nurses in the emergency room that we were on our way. We arrived and were soon led to the "psych room," where these patients are separated from all the other patients. We were in a small room off the beaten path. My father immediately sensed that he was different.

The psychiatric resident interviewed my father. This time, my father didn't start with "my wife died." Instead, he began with, "Gizi, who was with me for five years, left me. It was a terrible shock."

I believed him this time, but I also knew that he had no idea what he was in for. The truth is that other than my few weeks of psych rotation in nursing school, I didn't know either. I was sure that he, and therefore I, was getting help for the first time. Real help. Help he so desperately needed. I wasn't optimistic that he could change much, but I hoped that maybe they could blunt his personality. It was obvious to me by now that if six Hungarian caretakers could not succeed, then having someone live with him was not an option and he would have to adapt to life in an independent living facility. His personality needed to be tamed.

After spending most of the day in the emergency room, we were finally taken up to the psych ward, a locked unit. My father could sign himself in, but he was not leaving easily. The rest of the hospital had recently been modernized, but not the psych ward. It was obvious that this ward was not their moneymaker. It was dreary. The hospital had no desire to make it a pleasant place and entice anyone to stay awhile or come again. We were led to my father's room. I said good night to him as he climbed into the bed, exhausted from the day, and I told him that I would be back the next day.

I don't remember if it was the second or third day of his stay that I received a surprise phone call from my father.

"Can you bring me my blue, double-breasted jacket with the handkerchief in the lapel pocket?" he asked.

This seemed a strange request from a depressed man in a psych ward. I thought maybe the antidepressants had kicked in, but this reaction seemed drastic and too soon.

"Sure," I said, "but why?"

He explained, "They have a group here, and they were fascinated by me. They listened to all my stories. In fact, my appetite is back, and I ate for the first time today. People are getting dressed nicely for the day. They are not in their pajamas. They have all sorts of activities here." He then proceeded to give me a list of clothes that I should bring him.

The next day, I arrived with the double-breasted jacket and his other requested clothes to find him lying in bed under a blanket, wearing his green ski cap, looking extremely depressed. It wasn't good. The green ski cap was never a good sign.

"I brought the double-breasted jacket," I said cheerfully.

He looked at me and in a flat, monotone voice said, "Take it back. Take it all back. I don't want any of it to stay here." He pulled the blanket closer to his face.

For the next three weeks, he flipped back and forth on any given day from extreme optimism to sullen depression. Mostly he was severely depressed. The psych ward was not what I would consider "therapeutic," but being confined and having his medications adjusted held a lesson for him that was therapeutic in itself. He didn't eat, but when he did, he was only allowed to eat in the dining room. In the dining room, he refused to sit down or look at anyone, so the staff set a place for him at a table by himself where he faced the wall. He took a few bites and was done. He was allowed to spend most of his day in bed, wearing the same clothes for four to five days, rarely showering, and seldom participating in ward activities.

Over the first two weeks, I visited daily, but during the last week, I skipped days because I needed to and because I believed that my father needed to adjust to my not being there. As a visitor, I had to ring a bell and announce who I was and who I was going to see before they would buzz me in. This particular nurse waited for me on the other side of the door to give me a ten-minute report whether I wanted it or not. I heard about every detail of his day: how she intervened, how important it was for me to visit my father often, and how he wanted to live with me and have me take care of him "the way he had taken care of me as a child." *Go to hell, you damn moron,* I thought. *You have no idea who this man is, so don't judge what he deserves.*

I rarely had a chance to speak with his psychiatrist during the hospitalization. I felt compelled to convey an accurate portrait of who my father really was, not an "ordinary" depressed person dealing with his recent losses.

Dr. S., my father's regular psychiatrist, was away one weekend, and another psychiatrist covered for him. He saw my father on Saturday and then again on Sunday. By Sunday, he was perplexed.

He called me on the phone and said, "I don't understand. Your father looked great yesterday, joking with me, telling me stories about himself. He was dressed, out of bed, and eating. Today he's in his pajamas and refusing to get out of bed, eat, or talk to anyone. He keeps saying that he wants to die."

I told the doctor that this had been the pattern since he first entered the hospital and that I was on my way over. When I arrived at the hospital, the doctor was waiting for me at the nurses' station. I gave him a synopsis of my father's personality.

"He sounds like he could be psychotic," said the doctor. "Does Dr. S. know any of the things that you are telling me?"

"I'm not sure," I replied. "In the past, I've offered to give Dr. S. information about my father, but he never seemed too interested. Now, I feel I have to."

I wanted to make sure that my father would get the right treatment. It was easy to believe that he was depressed over losing his wife and his companion, but I knew better. These events were only a small part of his condition.

I called Dr. S. the next day and said that I believed there was much more to my father's condition that he needed to know. I was hoping, of course, not to offend him or have him think that I doubted his ability to deduce a diagnosis from my father's presentation, but I knew there was a great deal that he hadn't heard or seen. To my advantage, Dr. S. had observed my father's erratic behavior and drastic mood swings. I hoped he would welcome the additional information that I could contribute.

"Can you please meet with me because I am not sure that you are getting the full picture?" I asked.

"I don't really have time available in my schedule," he said, "except for a half hour tomorrow."

"I'll take it," I said.

I arrived at Dr. S.'s office the next day to find him running late. He informed me that he actually only had twenty minutes for me. I have never spoken so quickly and so persuasively with so few words. I carefully selected themes that would signify something more than "typical depression associated with grief." I needed to convince him that my father had a serious personality disorder.

"Dr. S.," I began, "you don't know about his sadistic behavior, the paranoia, yelling 'communist whore' at relatives, eavesdropping, forbidding relatives to visit, locking and double locking his room, placing oven grills and bells in the windows, sleeping on an army cot, making me promise as a child that I wouldn't circumcise my future sons, living in solitary confinement, wearing the favorite forty-year-old blue shirt that he rarely took off or washed, collecting rubber bands, hoarding food ..."

Please, please, I thought, *listen to me. This is no ordinary man.* I knew that if he heard me out, he would be convinced and would help my father and me with this lifelong burden.

Finally, Dr. S. said, "He sounds delusional, maybe even psychotic."

Relief flooded through me.

Dr. S. and I quickly decided that my father was going to move into an independent living facility. My main goal was to make it work. My father needed to be medicated enough so that he would get along in society. We agreed to keep him on the antidepressants, hoping that it would be enough.

My father did not want to hear about the independent living facility, but he desperately wanted out of the unbearable situation on the psych ward. After three weeks, he was convinced that he would never be allowed to leave. He was not oblivious to his surroundings. He saw the suicide watches, the self-mutilators, the sad and lonely, and the psychotics. He wanted out. When I arrived one day, I found him lying in bed with the green ski cap on his head and the blanket pulled up to his chin.

"Do you think I will ever get out of this place?" he asked me.

"I'm looking into it," I said, thankful that I had him in a vulnerable position but also perplexed by his question.

"Are you ready to look at the assisted living brochure?" I asked.

I took out the same brochure that he had refused to look at a few days earlier. I sensed he was giving up the fight and was ready to go. Anywhere would be better than the psych ward.

The social worker from the psychiatric ward and the physician from the independent living facility were to evaluate him to see if he was fit to live there. I held my breath as they made their assessment. Thankfully, they accepted him.

The new living facility had very welcoming staff members. They asked me about his interests so that they could make the transition easier for him. I was grateful to them but still skeptical. I knew my father. I had never known him to have any friends or get along with anyone, except for Levi Weiss in Israel and a religious Norwegian man he had worked with named Chris Hendrikson. Somehow his relationship with Chris was a relationship that my father respected and didn't sabotage. Chris was an unusually kind and accepting person.

My father left the hospital, twenty-one days after he was admitted, I asked my husband to meet me. Karen, the activities director, who was also the daughter of Hungarian Holocaust survivors, took my father by the arm as she spoke the few words of Hungarian that she knew, and she led him to the baby grand piano. His face lit up. He played a tune on the piano, and I couldn't believe my eyes. He was connecting. I took him down to his room as Karen called after him, saying that he would have to come back and entertain them with more piano music later. We went through the admission procedure and got my father settled in. He said that he was tired and wanted to go to bed. With unanticipated relief, we left.

The next day, I received a phone call at work from the social worker. "Your father is not doing too well. You need to come because he is sitting in the corner of the living room, refusing to speak, and saying over and over again that he wants to die."

I phoned my husband and told him that he had to come with me because I knew—and he knew, and I was sure my also father knew—that I could not be tough enough on my own. I waited in the parking lot of the facility until my husband arrived so that we could walk in together. Gary was his usual, confident self. He was going in with a mission to accomplish.

I looked at Gary and said, "Please don't be mean."

"Do you want me to handle it or not?" Gary asked, which of course, I did.

We walked in through the lobby and were greeted by Lynn, the house social worker.

"He's in there," she said, pointing to the common living room where he had joyfully played the piano the day before.

This time, the piano was quiet, and the air was thick. We followed Lynn into the room. Curled on a chair in the left corner was my father, expressionless and wearing dark sunglasses. He wore his winter coat and the green ski hat. He was wrapped in a fleece blanket.

Like a three-year-old left in nursery school for the first day, he said, "I don't want to stay here. I don't like it here."

"Abba, let's go to your room so that we can talk," Gary said.

My father adamantly refused to leave the communal living room and go back to his room. He repeated again and again that he did not want to stay there and that he wanted to die.

To my embarrassment at what I'm sure seemed heartless to the people who didn't know the lifetime of pain my father had inflicted on his family, Gary said very loudly, "Abba, you are not coming to live with us. We know that's what this is all about, and it won't work. Living with us is not an option."

I was so thankful to my husband.

"Abba," Gary continued, "if you don't want to stay here, then let's go back to the psychiatric ward right now. Maybe that's where you still belong."

My father knew that Gary meant business. He agreed to go back to his room on the condition that he would not be alone. We hired a home health aide to stay with him.

As we walked out of the building, Gary turned to me and said, "He looked like a homeless person in there."

We spent the next few days making daily phone calls to my father and visiting him. I held my breath each time the phone rang, hoping that his stay would work out and at the same time doubting it because of his history.

Vicki assured me that the staff had seen it all and that they would be able to handle him. I desperately wanted to believe it. If he could be medicated enough to pass for normal, it would be enough. Phone calls from the facility social worker and manager came almost daily. I weaned my visits to twice a week, which, of course, my father didn't like.

After a few days, he got aggravated with the aide who "did nothing but talk on the phone." He asked to get rid of her, so we did. Next, on the advice of the social worker to help my father adjust to living there, I made arrangements to have the nurses assist him with his medications. I also made arrangements for a male aide to assist him with his laundry and supervise him during his showers.

Roland, the male aide, was a large, gentle, black man from Ghana. He was roughly six feet tall and weighed three hundred pounds. There was a misunderstanding about my father paying him to do the laundry, and my father complained to the manager, who repeated the complaint to Roland. From that point on, my father was petrified of Roland and accused him of coming into his room. He called Roland "The Intruder" or "The Big G" (for *gorilla*), and he repeatedly accused Roland of coming into his room, moving things, and drinking his soda. My father showed me the evidence each time I visited. "You see this?" he'd say, "I didn't leave it here. It was The Intruder. He was in my room again."

I could have ignored these outbursts, but unfortunately, my father was so convinced of what he believed that he filed several complaints with the social worker and the manager. He claimed Roland came into his room and took his stuff. He presented his complaints in writing, threatening to write down details of what Roland did in his room as proof. I thought, *Oh, great. The only proof they will have is that my father is bizarre.*

My father put furniture in front of his door to prevent The Intruder from coming in. He put a sign outside his door that read, *I know who you are, and so do the police. They are watching you.*

The phone calls erupted again. The house manager would go into his room, see the pile of furniture, and give me a phone call. One day, I got a call from the manager: "We were in your father's room. He has put all his furniture in front of the door. It's really dangerous, and we can't allow him to do that."

My first thought was *Go in there and tell him,* but I knew his behavior was my burden. The manager and staff had been extremely tolerant and accepting. I promised to come after work. I drove up the Palisades Parkway to Exit 4 and thought to myself, *That's it. I've had it. He requires more energy than my three kids, my husband, and my dog combined. He requires more work than my mother did for three years with terminal cancer, chemotherapy, and radiation. He is relentless and will kill me before he dies himself. He deserves the same from me that he gets from my sister and brother: nothing.*

I had reached my limit. I arrived at the home and marched straight to his room, but he was not there. I went to find Christine, the manager. She agreed to open the door to his room so that I could take a look. Furniture—every last piece of it—was piled ten feet deep against the door. The kitchen table, four chairs, a recliner, two living room chairs, and anything else he could manage to drag over. I thanked Christine and assured her that I would handle the situation.

When I found my father walking around the hallways, I said, "Christine showed me your room. We need to talk. Let's go back to your room." We walked in silence back to his room.

I closed the door and said, "You need to listen to me very carefully now. I'm not sure you understand, but there are rules here, and the rules say that you may not block your door. You may have one kitchen chair in front of the door, but that is it. Nothing else. You need to understand that if you don't live by their rules, you will not be allowed to live here. The only other option for you is to live in a psychiatric facility for the rest of your life, so you need to decide. Look around. Do you want to live with these people for the rest of your life or with the kind of people you saw in the psychiatric unit? Those are the choices."

He stared at me deep in thought. With a troubled look, he said, "Everyone knows that The Intruder is coming into my room and taking my stuff. I wrote down every detail and gave it to them, and they believe me."

"No one believes you," I said. "No one believes that

someone is coming in here. You are moving things and forgetting. They don't believe that anyone is coming in here."

"Then why don't they tell me that?" he asked.

"Because they are nice," I explained. "They don't want to upset you. They don't believe that someone is taking your stuff, but they understand that you believe someone is."

He looked at me like a confused little boy.

I met with Vicki and Lynn, the two social workers who had been dealing with him, and we devised a plan. We agreed that I would limit my phone calls and visits. He and they would stop calling me at work unless it was an emergency. Vicki, the outside social worker, would be the first contact person unless it was a medical emergency. He would be allowed to install a door alarm, put locks on his closets, and place one chair in front of the door. We met with my father and discussed the plan. He agreed to it. I bought padlocks for his closets and installed them. He tied a few empty water bottles to his door for added security and even put a cord with a lock around his refrigerator so that he could keep The Intruder out of his stuff. It worked for everyone.

THE LETTER

To persuade my father to try out the independent living facility, I had promised not to give up his rental apartment for a few months in case the new facility didn't work out. I knew the apartment was not an option because he was incapable of getting along with a housekeeper. And he was not going to step foot in my house. I had finally come to my senses.

To my surprise, one day, as I gingerly reminded him how much the other apartment was costing each month, he said, "Get rid of it."

"Are you sure?" I asked.

"I'm sure," he said.

I immediately called the realtor to terminate his lease. Little by little, I went through his belongings and cleaned out his apartment. It felt as though I was unfolding his life. I had access to his most private things. I opened his desk drawer, and there was Book Number Two, the composition book where he had meticulously tracked all his ailments. Underneath that notebook was Number One, the composition book where he tracked my mother's weekly allowance and the pennies he had given us. To the right of every entry was my signature, which I can clearly trace back to my teen years. Occasionally, my sister had also signed the entries. On one line under a column labeled *Expenses*, it read, *Birthday present for Kathy, $30*. Next to it was my obligatory signature on October 31, 1972, my fourteenth birthday. There were signatures for ten-dollar dental visits and nine-dollar doctor appointments and the famous "Christmas present" that my sister and I had been so disappointed by. Everything was documented.

Then I spotted the double lock that he had used all those years to keep us out of his room. There were also photos, one of which showed my sister and me with the "funky bikes." As I sifted through the boxes of envelopes, one caught my attention. It was labeled *Keti's Surgery*. I opened it to find the operative reports and bills associated with my abdominal surgery in 1975. I noticed another envelope with an enclosed letter addressed to my father. I turned the envelope over, and the return address read *Dr. E. L. Hofstader, Scarborough, Ontario*. I was in disbelief. I had never heard of such a person or any other Hofstadter.

I took the letter to Gary and said, "You're not going to believe this. I think my father has a cousin in Canada. This cousin must know him well because he refers to my father as Laci, his Hungarian nickname."

I was excited. There was a chance that I could meet someone new from my father's family. There was a chance that this person knew my father before the war and could disclose what he was like before the traumatic events of his young adulthood.

On my next visit to my father, I confronted him: "I found a letter sent to you when I had surgery in 1975 by a Dr. Imre Hofstader. Who is he? Is he related to you?"

"Yes," my father said. "He is my first cousin. He is the son of Uncle Villi, who visited us when we lived in Israel. Most likely, you wouldn't remember because you were very young."

He was right. I did not remember meeting an Uncle Villi, although I vaguely remembered hearing of him. The next time I visited my father, I brought the photograph of my father's grandfather Lieb and his four sons: Moishe, Villi, Armin, and Jeno.

I said, "I'm trying to record the family history. I think it is important for you to tell me what happened to them so that our family has the information for generations to come."

This time, he didn't reject my request:

"Wildheim [Uncle Villi]," he said, "is the father of Emeric who goes by the name Imre, the doctor from Canada whom you referred to, and Sanyi, who is also in Canada. Uncle Villi survived the Holocaust, but barely. After being liberated from the camps, Imre and Sanyi took their father by the arms, one on each side supporting him because Uncle Villi hardly had the strength to stand on his feet. He was half dead. The second one is my father, Moishe. He was taken first to the forced labor camps and then most likely to the concentration camps, because he was never heard from again. The third is Armin. He also survived and moved to Canada. The forth, Jeno, was in Mauthausen with Uncle Villi, Imre, and Sanyi. He had a wife, Ilonka, and four beautiful, young daughters: Clara, Marta, Vera, and Kato. His wife and four daughters perished in the Holocaust. When Jeno was liberated from Mauthausen with Uncle Villi, Imre, and Sanyi, he knew that his wife and daughters had been killed. His condition was very bad. He just lay on the ground in despair over his family's demise and refused to move. He died within a few days."

I saw my father's pain and knew that it was time to stop, but I could not rest until I had more information about Imre. I Googled him and went to the medical library at work, looking for some clue. I searched for him as an individual and searched for the medical facility listed on the envelope's return address. I came up with nothing. I gave up, disappointed, not knowing where else to look, and justifying my defeat with the idea that whoever he was, he was most likely no longer alive.

A few weeks later, I had a lunch date with my friend Myra Levy, an Israeli, who was relentless in her quest for information. She had found the information about the *Rafiach*, the ship that sank while my mother was on board. Myra tirelessly surfed the Web and was a true sabra in her assertiveness.

As we sat at Café Angelique in Tenafly, we talked over our Israeli sandwiches.

"How are you doing with your book?" Myra asked.

"I'm just about done, but there is one stone left unturned."

"What is that?" she asked.

I told her about the envelope and Imre.

"If Imre is still alive," I told her, "he might be able to provide me with crucial information regarding my father's prewar character."

In her usual, self-confident manner and without a hint of doubt in her voice, Myra said, "Give me his name and all the information you have. I will find him for you."

That evening around nine, I got into bed to watch alittle television. The phone rang, and when I answered it, I heard an overexcited Myra.

She exclaimed, "You're not going to believe this! I found him! I found him! He called me, and I spoke to him. Hang up the phone! He is calling you right now!"

With Myra in the middle of a sentence, the call-waiting beep sounded. I had barely processed what Myra was telling me. Stunned, I pressed the button to bring the other call through.

A calm, kind voice at the other end of the phone line said, "Good evening. This is Imre Hofstader. Who are you?"

I froze for a minute, not knowing where to start. I feared rejection from this voice on the phone in the same way my father had rejected me so many times before. Maybe this man was happy to hear from me, but maybe he was like my father and would not want anything to do with a stranger.

I said, "My name is Kathy Hoffstadter-Thal. I am the daughter of Laci Hofstadter."

After briefly pondering the name Laci Hofstadter, he said, "I don't know who that is. Let me think."

"My mother was Luizi," I quickly jumped in. "You and my father are first cousins. My father's father was Moishe Hofstadter."

"Oh yes, I know who he is. You are his daughter?" he asked.

"Yes," I replied.

I told him that until I had found the letter and the envelope a few months ago, I had never heard of him or almost anyone else from my father's family.

"Is your father still alive?" he asked.

"Yes," I said.

"Is he well?"

Not sure how to answer this question and trying to be sensitive but not deceitful, I said, "Yes, he's physically well. Mentally, though, he's not a hundred percent."

I told Imre that I was writing my memoirs and that I knew very little about my father, his family, or his wartime experiences because he never talked about any of it. I told him that I was very eager to hear about what my father was like as a child.

"I can't really say," he said, "because I met him for the first time shortly before the war." Imre explained that most of the Hofstadters lived in a Hungarian town called Mezokovesd. I knew that my father had lived in both Kishkunhalas and Nagyteteni.

"Your father came to visit our grandfather, Lieb, who lived near us, and that was when I met him. He seemed like a nice, bright guy. He became a teacher, right?"

"No," I said. "He was studying to be a teacher, but the war interrupted his studies, and he never finished."

I tried again, "What about his brothers?"

"Brothers?" he asked, confused.

"Yes, brothers," I repeated. "Well, actually, I'm not sure that there are brothers because for years my father told me that he had one brother who was killed in the war, but more recently, he told me that he had two brothers and that one survived the war but was killed in a mining accident in Canada, so I am somewhat unsure myself."

"I only know of a younger brother," he said. "He was hospitalized in Montreal with schizophrenia. The last that my brother and I heard about him was in 1975."

I was sure I misheard him. I tried to continue the conversation in a friendly, matter-of-fact tone so that this newly found loved one wouldn't back away.

"Is he still alive?" I asked.

"I don't know, but probably not," he said.

"Do you know his name?" I asked.

He thought for a minute before responding, "No, I can't say that I do remember. Maybe my brother does."

"Does Janus or Stephan sound familiar? Those are the names that my father told me."

"No, those don't sound familiar," he said. "And both those names would be hard for me to believe because they are not Jewish names. Most Jewish people in Hungary at that time gave their children Jewish names."

I put the shocking words aside, knowing that there was too much for me to sort out at the moment. I would have to deal with the truth and significance of his words later.

"My brother, Sanyi, is still alive," Imre continued. "He also lives in Canada, not far from me, in Toronto. We are very close."

That statement was hard for me to imagine: members of my father's family could like each other and be close.

Imre went on, "My brother is religious, but I am not. I have two daughters and five grandchildren. My brother has a lot of grandchildren. I can't say for sure how many, somewhere around twenty-five. He already has several great-grandchildren.

"Would it be OK if I come to visit you sometime?" I asked boldly.

"That would be very nice. You can stay in our house and meet the family."

"That's very nice of you," I said.

It was a far nicer thing to hear than anything my father had ever said to me. The conversation was hard for me to process. Imre was warm, friendly, caring, giving; these attributes were hard to accept. My father's world was always about him: "I need . . . ," "Bring me . . . ," "Can you . . . ?" He never thought or did for anyone else. Not his wife, not his children, not his grandchildren. But here was a man who was related to my father and was offering hospitality, kinship, and the type of kindness I had never known from my father.

We talked for a few minutes about the different spellings of our last name and how the changes had come about. Even he and his brother had two different spellings.

"You know," he said, "we are related to some pretty famous people. Have you ever heard of Richard Hofstadter, the historian? Or Robert Hofstadter, the Nobel Prize-winning physicist?"

I had. Throughout the years, I had often been asked if I was related to them. I once asked my father if we were related to them. He said that he believed they were distant relatives.

Imre continued, "My grandfather, who is your great-grandfather, Leon [Lieb] Hofstadter, and Richard's father were brothers. I am not sure of our exact relationship to Robert. There is also a New York Supreme Court judge named Samuel Hofstadter to whom we are related."

As Imre spoke, the word *we* resonated in my ear. I was part of this family at last. Finally, I was a member of the family for which I had longed since my earliest days.

He added, "But I believe the judge, like some of the other Hofstadters, converted to Christianity after the war."

It was getting late, so I said goodbye and told him that I looked forward to meeting him and the family.

"My husband and I will plan a weekend to come visit you in Canada," I said with eagerness.

"We would be delighted to meet you," he said with sincerity.

As I hung up the phone, I began to process the information I had just received. Brother. Schizophrenic. 1975. Still alive. Montreal. So close. And then I had a flashback to something that I had suppressed or simply dismissed as delusional: the day thirty years ago when I had walked past my father's room and heard him crying.

I thought some more. His brother, whose name I still didn't know, born in 1927, would have been around seventeen in 1944, when most Hungarians were taken to the camps and when his mother and brother were killed. He was eighteen at the end of the war, the same age as my oldest son, Adam. My heart ached with the thought of him being alone all those years. How could my father, who always cried "poor me," leave a brother ten years younger without ever looking back? How could he have disposed of his brother like that? I was sickened by these thoughts. I began to wonder about this mysterious brother. What kind of life had this man lived? Was he alone? Did he have family? Perhaps he wasn't schizophrenic at all. I had read of holocaust survivors labeled as schizophrenic and destined to a lifetime of psychiatric hospitals when in fact they were not schizophrenic. They had been labeled as such in an era before much was known about post traumatic stress disorder.

THE TRUTH BEGINS

On the next trip to the psychiatrist with my father, he spoke in the car about the school he had gone to. He had been reminiscing about his childhood more these days after I revealed to him that I had contacted his cousins in Canada.

"You can find my name on the list in the Polgaris School in Hungary—me and my brothers," my father said proudly.

"Brothers? Or brother?" I asked.

"Brothers," he said.

"And what were their names again?" I asked, remembering what Imre had said to me about Janus and Stephan not being Jewish names.

"OK, I didn't tell you the truth before. Their names were Imre and Artur," he confessed.

"And how old were they?" I continued.

"Imre, born in 1923, was three years younger than I was. Artur, born in 1927, was ten years younger than I was."

I thought, *Great, my children were named after his brothers as a tribute to them and to honor him, and my father had allowed me to give my sons fictitious names!* Jonathan's name was not a problem because he was named after Janus as well as Gary's grandfather Jacob, so the *J* was justified. But Adam's middle name was Stephan. There were no other *S*'s in the family, and after all, the significance of it was totally lost. I would need to give some thought to keeping the name.

We arrived at Dr. S.'s office. I took my usual spot in the waiting room chair as Dr. S. came out to call my father into his office. As they walked down the hall, my father tried to charm the psychiatrist with his usual conversations about religion and philosophy.

"Dr. S.," I heard my father ask, "you are a rabbi, right?"

"Right," said the doctor.

"Do you know what they say about doctors in the Torah?" my father asked.

"No, what do they say?"

"*Tov shebarofim lagehinom.* The best of the doctors can go to the hell," my father said as he chuckled and shuffled down the hall.

This time, the psychiatrist unintentionally left the door between the waiting room and his office ajar. I could hear the conversation between them.

"Dr. S.," my father began, "do you know why I come here to see you?"

"Yes," answered the doctor.

"Why?" My father asked.

"Because you are depressed," said Dr. S.

"No, that is not why," my father said. "It is because my house in Brooklyn was a marijuana dance. The three children made my life so miserable. It was unbearable. I don't want to say too much about the children because I don't want to damage their reputations, but believe me, they made my life hell!"

Hearing those words, I felt the rage begin to build inside me. *How dare you,* I thought. *How dare you, the one who destroyed our childhoods, your wife, your marriage, our family and left your brother by the wayside, turn it around to put the blame on us?*

The doctor called me in for the last few minutes, as was our usual routine.

"Your father looks great," Dr. S. said.

"Yes, he does," I said.

TORONTO

Gary and I planned a trip to Toronto for the first weekend in August, the same weekend that we would be visiting the kids at sleepaway camp. We had never been to Niagara Falls, so we arranged to go there as well. I telephoned Imre to give him the dates.

"Sanyi wants to take us all out to dinner," Imre said. "We should also include Judit, your father's other cousin. She would be very insulted if she was not included. She is also writing her memoirs, so I am sure that she will want to meet you. You will have a lot in common. Did I tell you that Sanyi's son-in-law also wrote a book on the Hofstadter family?"

"No," I said.

"Well, he did. It was self-published, but it's really just for the family," Imre explained.

"I will ask him if you can have a copy."

I was excited. We agreed on the dates.

"We have a big house. You'll stay with us," Imre offered.

I thanked him, but I told him that we preferred to stay at a hotel.

"I can understand. You don't really know us," he said.

On August 2, 2007, Gary and I visited the boys at camp in the Poconos. We kissed the boys goodbye and left for my much-anticipated journey. When we arrived at the hotel in Toronto, I telephoned Imre.

"Sophie and I will pick you up at three o'clock. Then, we will show you around Toronto. At five, we will meet Sanyi and Judit at the restaurant," he said.

By 2:45 p.m., I was getting very nervous. Gary announced that he was going down to the lobby "just in case they have trouble finding us." *Don't leave me,* I thought to myself, but I knew better than to say it. He walked out of the room, and I paced back and forth as I repeatedly asked myself, *I wonder what he looks like? Will he like me? Will he think I'm pretty enough? Smart enough?* Gary came upstairs. It was 3:45 p.m., and they were forty-five minutes late.

"Hungarian time," Gary joked as the phone rang. He picked it up and said to the person on the other end of the phone, "We will be right down."

I took a deep breath to brace myself.

When we arrived downstairs in the hotel lobby, a sweet looking, finely dressed, older gentleman waited calmly by the front desk. He was the first person in my father's family that I had laid my eyes upon in my conscious memory. I was forty-eight, and the last encounter, I had had with a member of my father's family, was at the age of six or seven. We introduced ourselves with first a handshake and then a gentle hug. It was a warm, familiar embrace, creating an immediate bond between us. It was the kind of familiarity that we naturally have with those who are connected to us. Imre smiled and led us to the car where his wife, Sophie, waited.

"Since it is a little late, we will go to our house for a quick drink, and then we can go to Sanyi's."

We drove to their home. Imre asked if I would like a rum and coke. I replied that I have never actually had one.

"You will have to try one then," he said.

Imre went into the kitchen to make our drinks as Sophie showed us around their home. I scanned each room, desperately looking for something familiar, something to make us "officially related." I spotted Herend figurines and doilies, and then there it was that something that I had been searching for, what every Hungarian home I had ever known had: plastic slipcovers.

As Imre came into the room holding the rum and cokes, I said, "Yes, I can tell that this is a Hungarian home. You have doilies and slipcovers."

They both looked at me perplexed, and Sophie told a long story about the chairs and how they had bought them during their travels to China. But it wasn't the history of the chairs or the exotic travels that I was interested in. It was the connection.

We sipped our rum and cokes as we snacked on cheese and crackers. I pulled out the family pictures that I had removed from my father's photo album. Some of the people I could identify and some I could not. I hoped that Imre could tell if they were related to us.

The first photo was the one of my father's grandfather, Lieb, with his four sons, the one I had recently viewed with my father.

"Yes, I have that picture as well," Imre said, pointing to the picture on the wall of the family room where we were sitting.

We drove to Sanyi's house. Imre rang the doorbell. I waited nervously with Gary, Imre, and Sophie, with whom I had begun to feel comfortable. The door opened, and in the entranceway stood Sanyi, a friendly, pink-cheeked man, wearing a yarmulke. Next to him stood his wife, Iren. I was a little surprised by Sanyi. From our phone conversation, I was expecting a much older looking, stooped, ultra-Orthodox man with payot (side locks), but he appeared much younger and much less Orthodox than I had pictured him to be. Sanyi invited us in. He asked Gary a traditional Jewish question: "So what do you do?"

As Gary tried to answer politely, I impulsively and nervously interjected, "He's a bum," leaving Gary to defend himself as I followed Iren into the living room.

"I never imagined that you would be so beautiful," she said to me. I can't think of anything that could have had a more positive effect on me at the moment. We were invited to sit in the living room of this second doi-ly-and-Herend-stocked home, but as far as I could see, this one did not have plastic slipcovers.

Sanyi picked up a blue, hardcover book and handed it to me. The cover read, *Family Chronicles: Hofstadter*. I wanted to hug the book.

"Come with me," said Sanyi. "I want to show you something."

I felt special being invited to view something pri-vately. He led me out of the room with a firm squeeze of my upper arm, a squeeze that told me he was definitely related to my father.

We went into the dining room, where dozens of pictures stood neatly on top of a console. At first, he showed me one of himself with his first wife, Kitchi, who had died a few years earlier. The love in his eyes made it obvious that he missed her. He pointed at the picture of great-grandfather Lieb and his four sons.

I said, "Yes, I have the same picture in my pocketbook."

"Did you know he was a very religious man and a well-known cantor?"

"Yes, I know," I said.

He showed me a picture of my great-grandmother, Feige Leah Hofstadter, which I had never seen before. Sanyi then proudly showed off pictures of his four children, more than twenty-five grandchildren, and few dozen great-grandchildren.

We went back to the living room, where the others waited. Sanyi announced that we had reservations for six o'clock, but we would have to stop to see Agi, another Hofstadter first cousin, who was recovering from shingles. Bruchchu, Agi's sister from New York, had died a few weeks earlier, but Agi had not yet been told. The family was waiting for Agi to recover so that she would be well enough to sit shiva. Once again, I felt cheated by my father. First cousin. New York. Died two weeks ago. I could have had a relationship with her.

In her house, Agi half sat and half reclined on a settee in the grand entrance hall near a long spiral staircase to the floor below.

We greeted each other, and in front of the group, she looked at me and asked, "Can I ask you a qveshton?"

"Sure," I said.

"Promise me you von't be offended."

"OK," I said.

"Do you keep the Shabbat?" she asked.

I looked at Gary, hoping that he would rescue me from my interrogator, but he did not. I took a deep breath before I answered.

"Well, we try to light candles," I said.

I could tell from her expression that it was not the answer she wanted.

"But do you keep the Shabbat?" she repeated, more adamantly this time.

"No," I said, feeling hurt and rejected, although this was not new to me.

Growing up with an Orthodox family on my mother's side, I was used to this kind of religious segregation. I knew that she asked the question out of ignorance and did not mean to be malicious. I had long ago learned to accept it.

I felt dismissed by Agi, but I tried not to take it to heart. I had been accepted warmly by Imre, Sophie, Sanyi, and Iren, so much more than I had anticipated.

We began to talk about my father and his brother. Agi said a few words about my father's brother.

"Yes, his brother, Artur, survived the war," she said.

She mumbled something about an SS uniform when Sanyi walked in with Judit.

We introduced ourselves. Judit stared at me with loving, familiar eyes that overwhelmed me with kindness. Her warm expression reminded me of my mother. I sensed that Agi knew something more about Artur, so I tried to steer the conversation to where we had left off before the interruption. However, Sanyi announced that we would have to leave, or we would be late for the restaurant.

"Wait a minute," I said. "Agi was telling me about my father's brother. Agi, can you tell me more about Artur?"

Instead, Sanyi responded, "We really need to go now."

It seemed that I was being sheltered from something, that they all knew something but were not willing to talk yet.

At the restaurant, Judit looked at me from the other end of the table. It was heartfelt warmth, but I was confused because she didn't know me. We were bound by blood, though. She studied me intensely as she sat with Imre at her end of the table, speaking Hungarian. I sat with Iren and Sophie. Gary sat across from Sanyi. After dinner, Judit insisted that Gary and I come to her house for dinner the next night.

The next evening, Gary and I went to Judit's house for dinner. She handed me a copy of her memoirs to take home. As we sat for dinner, Judit went to the buffet and picked up an old, black-and-white, framed photograph of a woman. "Last night at the restaurant, I was looking at you, trying to figure out who you reminded me of in the family. When I got home, I realized it was Henusch (Hoinalka), my aunt who was killed in Auschwitz. She was your great aunt. I think you look a lot like her."

As we sat eating dinner, Judit told me the following about my father's brother:

"Yes, I remember Artur, your father's younger brother, very well. We were in Italy at the Zionist organization. My husband, Bill, worked in the office. One day, a new group of youngsters arrived, and someone ran into the office to tell us that a young man with the name Hofstadter had just arrived. I was excited to see who it was. I ran outside and saw that it was Artur. He was very good looking, with blond hair and blue eyes. I remembered most the way he carried himself, very self-confident. I was happy to have him there because he was family and because there were so few of us left. One day, someone said that Artur was playing cards, which was taboo. I wanted to see for myself, so I went to look. I needed to keep an eye on him because he was a young kid. I saw that he was playing cards, so I said, 'Artur, where you come from, it's not nice to play cards.' He answered, 'I wore a Nazi uniform. I know what to do. No one can tell me.' That was 1947. One day, he just disappeared."

After dinner, Gary and I were invited for dessert at Lily's, Imre's oldest daughter. Once again we received a warm reception. We were greeted by Imre; Sophie; Lily; Lily's husband, Jay; and Lily and Jay's teenage daughter, Jackie. Shortly after, Arlene arrived, Imre's younger daughter, with her husband, David. I was thrilled to meet this new family.

I told them a little bit about my father, not wanting to say too much so that I would not appear callous. I told them that I kept my maiden name because I had believed I was the last surviving Hofstadter. I believed that there was no one left except for my father, and because my brother had changed his last name, I felt obligated to preserve the family name. Imagine now finding out that there are dozens of Hofstadters! We laughed.

We then spoke about how I found Imre, and somehow the conversation veered toward my father's brother.

David, Arlene's husband, jumped up in excitement and asked, "Isn't he the one with the SS uniform?"

This was the third time I was hearing about Artur and an SS uniform.

"What else do you know?" I asked.

He answered that he didn't know any more, and I wasn't sure if he was telling me the truth or if he was responding to the unspoken pressure from the others in the room. Whatever the truth was, I didn't feel it was proper for me to be forceful during this initial encounter. We took a few pictures and said goodbye to my newly found family.

THE TRUTH CONTINUES

When I arrived back at my father's apartment, I said, "Daddy, there is talk in Canada of your brother being in an SS uniform. There is also talk of him being in a psychiatric hospital and that maybe he is still alive. I am asking you to please tell me what you know because I really want to know. As a matter of fact, I so desperately want to know that if you don't tell me, I will hire a private investigator."

He answered, "Be careful. Be careful of what you want to know."

He looked agitated, and I knew the limits. I would have to stop for now. I was almost certain that the story of the SS uniform was not true. Having an uncle in an SS uniform was too unimaginable, and if he actually was in an SS uniform, I would think that he wouldn't have bragged about it, especially to relatives and other survivors of the concentration camps. I wondered what my father knew, but like so many other things I wanted to know about, my attempt to uncover the truth would be futile. He would most likely never disclose the truth

The next time I came over, my father said, "I will tell you what happened to my brother."

"OK, let's hear it," I said, hoping it would be the truth.

For the first time, my father revealed the following information to me:

"I saw my brother after the war when I was walking through the streets of Budapest. I saw a young man walking with a sack of flour on his back. I looked up, and it was my brother, Artur. We called him Artie. We were so happy to see each other. He told me that in Nagyteteni, he saw the fascists come and take our mother away on a wagon. He couldn't help her. He had been sent to do forced labor in a textile factory and later stayed alive by hiding in the basement of a store and eating chocolate powder. We parted, and I didn't see him again until I was in Italy.

In Italy, he was at first with the Toronto group. He said they didn't really take him in, so he walked to the other end of Italy where I was staying. One day, he suddenly appeared. I let him stay with me and my group, and he was very happy with us. He had worked in Hungary as a commercial art apprentice, so he decorated the place with big, beautiful letters. He was very popular with the girls. It was not unusual to find him sleeping on the beach with a girl.

I had a girlfriend in our group. Her name was Sarah Kertes. My brother hoped that I would marry her, and then the three of us could live together as a family. But she had a venereal disease. Syphilis I think it was. She claimed to have been raped by a Russian soldier. I loved her, but I couldn't bring myself to marry her because of the syphilis. We all stayed together, first in Groto Forota and then in Ostia Lido De Roma, for about two months.

It was then that the two soldiers came and gave me the special assignment I told you about before, and I had to leave for Palestine. I said goodbye to Sarah and Artie. I told Artie that we would soon see each other again, but he was reluctant to go to Palestine. He said he didn't want to work with a hoe in the Negev. He had no interest in going there. His plan was to be adopted by my Aunt Malvin Shiffman's daughter, Elaine, and her son-in-law, Hugo, in Pittsburg. But when the time came, they were struggling financially and decided not to take him in. Instead, he went with the Jewish transport to live with an Orthodox Jewish family in Calgary, Alberta. They treated Artie as a son. The couple had a daughter who helped my brother learn English. They all seemed happy. New immigrants had to work in the coal mines for a year, so my brother was taken to work at the coal mines. Imagine, at nineteen years old, after going through the hell of hells during the Holocaust, and now he's in the coal mines. I received a letter from Artie in which he said that the Jews were hunting him. I wasn't really sure what he was talking about. Soon after, the woman from Calgary wrote me a letter and said that Artie had some sort of a mental breakdown in the coal mine. The workers called an ambulance and Artie asked the driver if he could stop at the families' house so that he could say goodby to them. The woman was heartbroken. She had tried really hard to give him a happy home but he seemed troubled.

I received a letter from a mental institution on LaSalle Boulevard in Montreal. It was from a doctor who was treating my brother. The doctor said that Artie was doing OK and that they even saw him smile for the first time. The doctor asked me to sign a letter stating that I would forward any restitution from my parents to pay for my brother's care. I signed it.

Uncle Villi came to visit us in Israel from Toronto. I asked him to help save my brother. He told me not to worry because my brother was in a sedated state. Soon afterward, I received a letter from my brother asking for pictures of you kids and saying that he would have to stay at the hospital for two years. He pleaded with me to get him out of that place, but I couldn't. I was sick myself, and my married life was hell. I never sent him the pictures.

The next letter I received from my brother was the last. In it, he asked me to send him a copy of the picture I had of our mother, and I never heard from him again. That was in the late 1950s."

I was pleased to get this new information from my father. When I arrived home, I went straight to the computer to Google the psychiatric facility on LaSalle

Boulevard in Montreal. It came up instantly: The Douglas Institute Mental Health Facility.

The next day, I telephoned the hospital and was transferred to the medical records department. I explained that I had just learned of an uncle who, to the best of my knowledge, was hospitalized there in the 1950s, and I said that no one in the family knew what had happened to him. I wanted to know if they had any information regarding his death, discharge, or the possibility that he was still alive and hospitalized. Being familiar with U.S. HIPAA patient confidentiality laws, I didn't think the answers would come easily.

"Are you the next of kin?" the woman who took my call asked.

"Well, officially, my father is, but he is eighty-eight and not capable, so yes, that makes me the next of kin," I said.

"Send us a letter stating that you are the next of kin and outlining the information you are requesting. Include everything you want because the hospital will only give you what you ask for."

"OK," I said.

I wrote down the address. It didn't seem too difficult. On my next visit to my father, I told him that I had contacted the hospital and that they were only willing to give out information about what happened to his brother to the next of kin.

"If I draft up a letter, will you sign it?" I asked, figuring I would have a better chance at getting information if my father officially signed the letter.

"I told you already. I know what happened to him."
He repeated the same story, ending with "The last time I
heard from him, he asked me to send him a copy of the
picture of our mother."

"Did anyone tell you that he died?"

"No," he admitted.

"Then how do you know he is not alive?" I asked.

"Because he asked me for the picture of my mother,
and I can only imagine why he was asking for it," he said.

"You think he wanted to kill himself?" I inquired
gently.

"Yes," he said.

"But you don't know for sure that he did, so will you
sign the letter?"

"Yes," he answered.

I drafted the letter, and on my next visit with my
father, I pulled it out of my bag.

"I have the letter for you to sign to get the information
about your brother," I said.

"I won't sign it," he responded. "I told you I know
what happened to him."

I had exhausted the issue. He was not going to
cooperate. I would have to act as the next of kin, so I
sent the letter declaring myself as such.

Two weeks later, the letter arrived from the Douglas
Institute. I was paralyzed. I could not open it. I handed
it to Gary. I watched as he read the letter, looking for any
expression on his face.

Gary read it out loud:

"Dear Mrs. Hoffstadter-Thal,

We acknowledge receipt of your request for information concerning your uncle, Artur Hofstadter. As all information concerning clients is highly confidential, I would like to cite Article 23: '... The heirs and legal representatives of a deceased user are entitled to be given communication of information contained in his record to the extent that such communication is necessary for the exercise of their rights in such a capacity.' ... Persons related by blood to a deceased user may be given communication of information contained in his record to the extent that such communication is necessary to verify the existence of a genetic or hereditary disease.' Therefore, in order to proceed with your request, kindly forward the following documents: proof of death, proof of the relationship to the deceased, and justification that the communication of this information is necessary."

Great, I thought. I knew "Prove that you are next of kin" had sounded too simple. I called the hospital and explained to the woman in medical records that my father, because of traumatic experiences in the Holocaust, was estranged from his brother. I asked if the hospital's letter was indirectly stating that his brother was dead.

"No," replied the woman. "It is a generic letter that we send to everyone who wants information."

She gave me the number for a government office in Quebec, where I might be able to get information regarding a death certificate if he was no longer alive. I contacted the Ministry of Justice (Directeur de L'état Civil) in Montreal. I was sent a form and a list of documents that I would have to provide. I included a copy of my father's birth certificate, my birth certificate, and a picture of Artur with the words *To my dear only brother, Laci* inscribed on the back in Hungarian. I hoped that these documents would be enough to produce a death certificate.

A few weeks later, the response came. Because I didn't have a date of death, I would have to file for an attestation, which would cost me approximately four dollars for each year I wanted to have searched. No problem. I wanted them to look as far back as 1950.

But they also wanted me to justify why I wanted the information. I was tired of all the roadblocks and again figured they would be more cooperative with my father's signature. I prepared the document and took it to my father. I knew that my request for his signature would have to be spontaneous. If I didn't have the document ready to go, chances are he would change his mind like he had done before.

When I walked into his apartment, I could see that he was in a fairly good mood.

"Daddy, I want to find out if your brother is dead or alive. I have the paper here to see if there is a death certificate. Will you sign it with me?"

"OK," he said, and he did.

Within two weeks, I received my response in the mail.

I braced myself as I sat down on the living room chair and opened the letter.

Madam,
We hereby attest that the death of Arthur Hofstadter appears on April 4, 2007, in Verdun, Montreal.

I was in shock. Artur had died exactly one year ago. I was too late. He had been so close for so long, and I didn't know it. Now, I would never have the chance to meet him. I wanted the letter to say that he had died twenty years earlier. Twelve months earlier was hard to except. His death occurred at what was almost exactly the time I found Imre.

I sat in the chair and cried and cried, holding the letter. I kept thinking, *How could this be?* I wept so loudly that Jonathan ran to the living room to see what was wrong.

"It's Abba's brother," I told him. "I just got a letter saying that he died a year ago. He was alive all these years with no one."

Jonathan knelt on the floor next to me, not knowing how to comfort me.

"I'm OK," I said. "I just need a few minutes alone to take it in."

He hugged me and went back to what he was doing. I sat and wondered, *How could my father's brother have lived six hours away from me most of my life without my knowing?* I was heartbroken. I hated my father. How could he have lied to me? How could he have simply dispensed with his brother?

ARTUR

I was distraught, but I could not stop until I found out more about Artur. Now that I knew he was dead, I was determined to find his burial site and any other information I could get about him. I tried that Douglas Hospital again, and I found the name and telephone number of the ombudsman this time. After many attempts, I got a response. I explained the story and gave her his date of death, hoping that she and others at the facility would communicate with me now that I had this new information. She said that she would see what she could find out.

A few days later, she called back and told me that Artur had a legal representative from the public curator's office in Quebec, named Elana Munoz-Bertrand, who could possibly help me. I realized, to my sorrow that if he had a legal representative, chances were that he did not have any family.

With persistence, I reached Elana Munoz-Bertrand, Artur's legal representative from the public currators office.

"Yes, I know who you are. I received you messages.

"Your Uncle Artur died April 4, 2007 at the Residence Yvon-Brunet where he lived for the last four years. It is a very nice place, one of the best."

"Do you remember him?" I asked.

"No, not really," she admitted.

"What was his diagnosis?" I asked.

"Schizophrenia," she answered.

"I am heartbroken over this situation. My father told me that his brother died in the 1950s in a coal mining accident. I would like to come to Montreal to get information about Artur from the Douglas Institute, see if there are any photos, and visit his grave."

The phone went silent.

"Are you still there?" I asked.

With a somber voice, she replied, "Yes, I am still here."

I knew what her silence meant.

"Was he cremated?" I asked, hoping and praying that the answer would be no but sensing that it would be yes.

"Well, I can't say for sure, but it says in his chart that he wanted to be cremated," she said.

"We are Jewish, you know. We don't cremate people," I said.

I wasn't sure why I was telling her that except that I had to say it out loud. My father did say that Artur converted to Christianity, but I was hoping it wasn't true. And if it was true, perhaps it was what he had to do to survive.

"As far as pictures, I may have one in his chart. There are two charts, one that I can view and one that I cannot. I'll look to see if there is a picture, and I'll call you back tomorrow," she promised.

I got off the phone and Googled the Residence Yvon-Brunet in Verdun, Montreal. It appeared on my computer screen with pictures. It seemed like an outdated assisted living facility, but it didn't look bad. There were nicely decorated rooms, a store, a café, and even a nursery school program. The picture that caught my attention was of the chapel. The room's focal point was a huge crucifix. There was a statue of Mary holding baby Jesus, and other Christian iconography. Residence Yvon-Brunet was clearly a Christian home.

After nearly two days spent anxiously awaiting Ms. Munoz-Bertrand's phone call, I realized that I could not go through the weekend without more information. In the late afternoon, I called her. Her answering machine had a long-winded message in French, so I called Myra to translate it.

"The message says that she will not be in for a few days," Myra told me.

I was crushed, but I had no choice except to wait longer. I left Ms. Munoz-Bertrand a message and sent her an e-mail saying that she had promised to get back to me and I was anxious to hear from her. To my surprise, when I checked my e-mail Monday afternoon, there was an e-mail from her. It read in part:

Madam,
Please note that the person responsible for
your father's [uncle's] file was Mr. Mario Biuzzi
at Center D'Hubergement Yvon-Brunet.

The e-mail included his telephone number and his
e-mail address. I immediately sent him an e-mail. The
next day, I telephoned Mr. Biuzzi.

"Yes, I received your e-mail. I have been gathering
things for you," he said.

He told me that he was responsible for the floor
where Artur lived for the last four years of his life and
that he knew Artur very well. I couldn't believe my ears.
He was the first person who could share something
about Artur's final years with me. I again rambled about
my father's deceit, his mental illness, how I would have
been there for Artur, should have been there for him,
and am now left sifting through pieces in an attempt to
make sense of a senseless situation.

"What do you want to know?" Mr. Biuzzi asked me.

"Tell me everything you know about my uncle. What
was he like?"

"OK, let me see what I have in his chart," he began.
"He was born in Austria; his father was a pastor. He
came to Canada via Italy at the age of sixteen with the
Jewish Youth Transport, although he was not Jewish.
They felt sorry for him, so they took him along with the
Jewish youth. That was in 1947. He was hospitalized at

the Douglas Institute for the first time in 1950, and then he was in and out until 1966. From 1966 to 2003, Artur was permanently hospitalized there."

He was not born in Austria. He was born in Hungary. And his father was not a pastor, he was a cantor," I said.

I wondered if Mr. Biuzzi was reading the wrong chart or if Artur had lied or if this delusion was merely part of Artur's mental illness. Whatever it was, I didn't want to jeopardize receiving more information from Mr. Biuzzi, so I quickly moved on.

"What was he hospitalized for?" I asked, recognizing that Mr. Biuzzi was eager to help.

"Schizophrenia," he answered. In 2003, he improved, so the hospital sent him to us at the Center D'Hubergement Yvon-Brunet."

"Did he speak French?" I asked.

"No, very little. He spoke German and Polish and a little English," he said.

"German and Polish?" I said, perplexed. "He was Hungarian. His main language was Hungarian. Did anyone know that?" Again, I wondered if this was a lie, a cover-up, or a reflection of his pathology.

"We had someone listen to him, and she said his languages were definitely Polish and German. They don't sound anything like Hungarian, so I am sure that the professional could tell the difference," he said. "I will finish putting together the package for you. I have a few pictures, and I will see what else I can find."

"That's very nice of you," I said, "but if it would be all right with you, I would like to come to Montreal to see you and the home, and I can get the pictures from you then."

"That would be fine," he said. "You can come whenever you like, and I would be happy to meet with you and show you around."

Two weeks later, I left for a three-day trip to Montreal by myself. I needed to do this on my own, in my own way, on my own schedule, and at my own pace. The Douglas Institute had refused to meet with me, so now I would at least meet with Mr. Biuzzi and try to find the mausoleum.

On Friday, I had an appointment to meet Mr. Biuzzi at noon. I followed the directions and could tell I was approaching the facility as I saw disheveled people on the corner of Newman Street. There it was. I recognized the building from the pictures on the Internet. I announced myself at the front desk and then sat down.

"Mr. Biuzzi will be with you in a few minutes," the receptionist announced.

Within a few minutes, a handsome, tall, clean-cut man in his late forties or early fifties introduced himself as Mr. Biuzzi.

"Come," he said, "let me take you upstairs to my office."

I sat down in the chair across from him. He picked up an envelope from his desk. It had *Mme Hofstadter* written on it.

"I have the pictures here for you," he said.

I panicked, not quite ready to see them. I took out the picture of Artur that I had brought with me, the one that he had sent my father from Italy right before he left for Canada, and handed it to him.

"Yes, that is Artie. I can see that," Mr. Biuzzi said. "He was very good looking."

I took out the picture of my father and handed it to him.

"Yes, they look very much alike," he said as he studied the picture.

"May I see the pictures?" I asked.

The envelope contained three pictures. I looked at each one intently and then hugged them close to my body as I wiped away tears. The images and the facts were hard to digest. Artur was so alive in the pictures, and for so many years, he was so close and so alone. I wanted to touch him, to hold his hand, to hug him. But it was too late.

Mr. Biuzzi handed me a tissue. He was sincere and compassionate even in his silent response. He didn't say anything. He sat quietly, waiting for me to finish processing what I had just seen. I felt his empathy.

I asked him again to tell me about Artur, and Mr. Biuzzi obliged. This time, the story was a little different, with a few more details:

"Artur was from Austria. His father was a Protestant pastor who helped the Jews escape from Austria. The

Nazis killed his father because he had helped the Jews. Because of what his father had done, a Jewish organization took Artur to Canada even though he wasn't Jewish. He was at the Douglas Institute from 1966 to 2003, and he did not do too well. When he improved, the doctors transferred him to us. He didn't talk much to anyone. He mostly liked the staff and didn't want to bother with the other residents. He ate at a table by himself because he didn't want to sit with the other residents. He didn't like to take his medicine, and he especially didn't like to take baths. He liked to wear the same clothes over and over again, and he especially liked to wear sweatpants and T-shirts."

I wondered again if Artur was psychotic or if he'd made up these stories to cover up his real identity. I knew that my father had belonged to the American Legion eventhough he had never served in the U.S. army. My father believed that since the Palmach was an American ally, he qualified. I often wondered myself if this was delusional or some ploy to be "protected" by the men in uniform in case the Jews were targeted again.

"Sounds a lot like my father," I said. "Did he ever mention his family?"

"No, never," he answered.

"What about things? Did he keep a lot of things? My father has a lot of things," I said.

"Oh, he didn't have much, but if he had something and lost it, all hell broke loose. For instance, he once found a quarter and held on to it day and night. One morning, he couldn't find it, and there was big trouble. We all looked around his room and under his bed, but we couldn't find it either. We put another quarter under the bed and pretended it was the one he had lost. He believed us and was able to calm down."

I thought, *If only I could have given him quarters.* I wondered what the real significance of the quarter was. What was he holding on to?

"Can you show me his room?" I asked.

"Absolutely. I can show you the rest of the place, too, if you'd like."

"Thank you. I would love to see it all," I said.

We walked out of his office, and he pointed to the seat directly outside his office door.

"This is where Artie sat almost every day, waiting to talk to me and to ask me for cigarettes," Mr. Biuzzi said.

We walked past the lounge, where a half dozen people sat smoking cigarettes. From there, we went to another, larger lounge.

"You see that chair near the window?" he asked. "That was his chair. He slept in that chair by the open window for hours."

I wondered if he had used a blanket when he slept. Did they know when he was cold? What was he looking at when he stared out the window all those hours? I was grateful to know that Artie was able to enjoy cigarettes, fresh air, and the friendship of this very kind man.

Next, we came to an elderly woman sitting in a wheelchair. She was slightly bent over, staring blankly at her wheelchair tray.

"She is Hungarian Jewish," Mr. Biuzzi said. "She had also been with Artie at the Douglas Institute. They came here together."

He knelt on the floor in front of her so that he could look up into her face.

"Masga," he said in a sweet, calm voice, "do you remember Mr. Hofstadter?"

She gave a little nod.

"What was his first name?" he asked her.

"Artie," she mumbled, her voice soft and raspy.

"Yes, that is right," he answered.

With those words, I took out the two pictures and placed them on her tray.

She pointed at Artur's picture and kept repeating, "Artie, Artie."

"This other picture is my father, Laszlo," I said. "He is Artie's brother."

She moved her head from side to side, studying the two photographs. She looked up at me, and I knew she understood. I placed my hand on her arm and found it hard to stop stroking her. I felt connected to Artur through her.

Mr. Biuzzi then took me to Artur's room. I stepped inside so that I could imagine him in it. It had a hospital bed and was hospital sterile.

"Would you like to see the rest of the home?" he asked.

"Yes," I answered.

We took the elevator to the basement. He showed me the garden room, the social hall, and the café where he took Artie for ice cream sundaes. And then we passed the chapel.

"May I go inside?" I asked.

"Of course," he said.

I looked around, and there was the Mary and Jesus statue and the large cross I had seen on the Internet.

Mr. Biuzzi must have read my face because he said, "You're uncle never really came in here. As a matter of fact, we have a priest and a rabbi, and Artie wasn't interested in either. He wasn't really interested in religion."

With those words, I thanked him for his kindness and left. I decided that even though no one at the Douglas Institute was willing to meet with me, I would go there anyway and walk the grounds. I needed to see it.

The main building was large and beautiful, with the words *Douglas Institute* on top. It was surrounded by smaller buildings and acres of property with metal sculptures in meticulously manicured gardens. It was obvious that the facility was well supported.

As I exited the parking lot, I saw a young man, who was clearly not a patient, walking toward his car. I asked him if he knew which building housed the patients. He pointed to a smaller building behind the main building.

I walked toward it and could see that it was behind a concrete wall. There was no one else in sight. There was an eerie silence. I suddenly had the bizarre feeling that I was in a Nazi ghetto. What was behind those walls? Why was it so silent? What was going on inside?

I walked a little farther to the gymnasium. It also appeared empty. I walked back toward my car and decided that I would try to get a look inside the main building. I went inside and asked the guard if I could use the restroom. He agreed and pointed a few yards down the hall. I walked slowly as I discretely read the door signs. There was one labeled *Rabbi*. The door was closed. I went to the bathroom and wrote down the rabbi's name. That information was for another day. Perhaps I could reach out to him one day in the hope that he would be empathetic and give me more information about Artur. I walked out of the building, and as I made my way back to my car, my cell phone rang. It was Ms. Munoz-Bertrand, Artur's legal representative. I had left her a message when I first arrived in Montreal, asking for Artur's burial site.

"Artur's ashes can be found at the Laval Cemetery in Laval," she said. I got in my car and drove straight to the cemetery.

The man at the cemetery office looked up Artur's name and directed me to a mausoleum. Inside were dozens of statues of Mary and Jesus. I walked up and down the aisles until I found the right aisle. And there, way up top, was a box with the name Artur Hofstadter on it. I went back to the office and asked the man for a piece of tape. I went back inside and found a rolling ladder to use to climb to the top. I pulled out the picture of Artur as a young adult that I had brought with me. I climbed up the ladder, kissed the picture, and taped it to his crypt. I promised to come back for him one day.

THE BLUE FISH

"I have pictures of Artur," I said to my father as we sat at the kitchen table. "Do you want to see them?"

"No," he said. He didn't say or ask anything about how I had acquired them although he knew of my recent trip to Montreal.

He sat at the table and cried "Poor little Artie!" In tears, he repeated some words in Hungarian that sounded something like "that sweet little child" to me. I found it hard to feel compassion for him. My father had lost any credibility of emotions long ago. I just sat there letting my father cry. I didn't say a word or reach out to touch him. I did feel sorry for him but, I could not bring myself to comfort him. He would have to deal with what he had created—the reality of leaving a young brother behind sixty years ago and never looking back. The sad reality was that my father was so damaged himself and he had struggled in his own life with mental illness. To have taken on a mentally disturbed brother was beyond his capability. I suddenly remembered when my father had been hospitalized a few years earlier on the psychiatric unit when he had asked me "Do you think I will ever get out of this place?" I was so baffled by the question at the time. I now realized that he feared suffering the same fate as his brother, Artur.

Sitting there it occurred to me that the man I feared for so many years was a frightened, fragile man. Despite the pain and suffering of my childhood, I felt sad for him. I knew that his character was not by choice.

A few weeks later, my father complained about being lonely.

"How would you like a fish?" I asked.

"That would be nice. A blue one," he requested.

On my next visit, I stopped at the pet shop to buy a bluish-red betta fish, a little fishbowl, colorful gravel, and plants. I placed the bowl and its contents on top of a bookshelf in his living room so that he could view it at eye level.

"I can't see it too well," he complained. "The bowl is dark. I'll go and get a flashlight so that I can see it better." A few minutes later, he returned with the flashlight and said, "Oh yes, now I can see it."

"His name is Sam," I said, hoping that if I gave the fish an identity, my father would be less likely to reject it.

A few days later, I called to see how my father and the fish were doing.

"The fish is not blue!" he exclaimed.

"It is," I said. "Look closer."

"The cleaning lady is here. I'll ask her," he said. "Felicia, what color is the fish?"

"Bluish-purple," she replied.

"It's not brown?" he asked.

"No," she answered, and he seemed satisfied with her judgment.

A few days later, I called him again.

"The fish doesn't like me," he said.

"What makes you think that?" I asked.

"He doesn't come near me when I go to his bowl," he explained.

"Fish don't usually come to people," I said.

"No, no," he insisted, "the fish doesn't like me because I probably went near it with the flashlight too many times. I don't want it anymore. Take it back."

On my next visit, I took the fish home and placed it next to Jonathan's other betta. I looked down into the bowl and thought, *Here you will be loved.*

Me and Imre at our first
meeting, Toronto 2007

Artur Hofstadter-
Italy after the War, 1947

Artur Hofstadter,
Montreal 2007

FAMILY MEMBERS MURDERED BY THE NAZI'S

Hofstadter Family

Irenke Hofstadter, P. 54

Feige Leah Hofstadter, p.54

Rochel Hofstadter, P. 54

Moshe Hofstadter, p.53

Jeno Hofstadter, p.53

Lieb Hofstadter, p.53

Clara Hofstadter-Jeno's child, p.54

Marta Hofstadter-Jeno's child, p.54

Vera Hofstadter-Jeno's child, p.54

Kato Hofstadter-Jeno's child, p.54

Imre Hofstadter

Hoinalka Hofstadter

Hoinalkas young daughter

Altman

Marie Altman Hofstadter, p.55

Rubenstein (Lili's husband), p.55

Lily (Rubenstein) Altman, p.55

Little boy Rubenstein, p.55

Bela Altman, p.55

Helen Altman, p.55

Little girl Altman (Helen & Bela's), p.55

Little boy Altman (Helen & Bela's), p.55

Ethel (Bruell) Altman, p.55

Elona (Altman) Daszkal, p.55

Aranka (Altman) Riener, p.55

Little girl Riener (Aranka's), p.55

Little girl Riener (Aranka's), p.55

Rubenstein (cousin), p.55

Rothfeld

Boreshka Rothfeld, p.12

Shanyi Rothfeld

Emil Rothfeld, p.13

Ester Rothfeld, p.13

Livia Rothfeld (Miklos's child)

Wife of Miklos Rothfeld

In memory of all the additional members of the Hofstadter, Altman and Rothfeld families whose names I did not include. They are not forgotten.

REFERENCES

1. My Father's cabin. http://www.britains smallwars. com/Palestine/providence/Providence.html. p.34.

2. Rafiah Pictures. http://www.palmach.org.il/show item.asp?itemId=6342&levelId=38530&itemType=0 &n=2. pgs. 57-58

3. The Hofstadter Chronicles, Photo of Lieb and Leah Hofstadter, pg 53 and The Hofstadter's, pg 54.